Uncommon Sense

Liam Sean

This book is dedicated to the memory of my Father, a Major and Combat Pilot in the United States Air Force, He remains my Hero.

Man knows no Master save creating Heaven,
Or those whom Choice and common Good
ordain.
-James Thomson
Liberty: A Poem 1736

We must learn to live together as brothers
or perish together as fools.
-Martin Luther King

What we do now echoes in eternity.

-Marcus Aurelius

CONTENTS

CHAPTER ONE

Intro

America. The dream. The idea. The freedom. The promise it holds, and the promise we make to America itself.

From many, one. Many, as in *all* of us; one, as in *together*. One nation, indivisible. Each of us is the firewall to keep this nation undivided. Each of us, while yearning to be free, also shines the light of liberty for our fellow citizens and citizens to be.

A nation founded on an idea must work to uphold that idea. Unlike any other form of government before America, the focal point of our Nation, of our unity, is nebulous, hard to hold, easily lost. Easily stolen.

We have reached the point in history where, as a Nation, we can choose to move forward with the great experiment of democracy, or we can succumb to oligarchy and dictatorship. The Shining City on the Hill, whose light is symbolized by the torch of the Statue of Liberty, is being extinguished in a powerplay of greed[1].

The choice is ours, as the inhabitants of America, as the defenders of freedom, as the stewards of this planet, as the guardians of truth. This is our time. Our legacy, what history tells of this time, must be the stuff of legend. Looming before us, uniting us, is the task of preserving democracy.

We cannot fail. There is too much at stake.

History is for reference, to learn from mistakes, to understand human nature, to see the course of events, to inspire. Do not dwell on it as hallowed. Do not set upon pedestals those who sought glory, riches, and fame, nor even those who sought truth and freedom. Emulate the positives from our shared history, learn from the mistakes. The heroes of America chose to dream, to endeavor, and to work. Some sacrificed all, so many could be free.

'The price of Liberty is eternal vigilance.'
-Thomas Charlton.

We are at a crossroads in the history of the United States. The road our Forefathers asked us to take involves bootstraps, sweat equity, and hard work. Work that often-times will seem unrewarding and frustrating. The other path is bright and shiny and lazy and appeals to our basest natures. It has been heavily researched, brightly packaged, and is instantly gratifying. It is also the path to oligarchy and eventually dictatorship.

Of the People, For the People and By the People means every single one of us. As the system has tilted in favor of corporations and the wealthy[2], as the disparity in wealth has become increasingly wide[3], the inalienable rights of Life, Liberty and the Pursuit of Happiness have become empty words. Servitude is not Life. Mass consumerism is no replacement for Liberty. Happiness should not be defined by super-sizing.

Reverend Vincent Harding said: 'The United States of America is a work in progress, a shadow on the wall of a multi-racial, compassionate democracy that does not yet exist.'

We are not looking for handouts. We are looking for a clear path on even ground. To ensure this, every single one of us must act, must work, must be the soil, the root, and the blade of democracy. It is from grassroots that mighty forests grow. The system is not perfect, but it still reflects this concept. The organizations exist, they are just waiting for you to join. *Your* vote, *your* wallet and *your* participation are the acorns that grow into mighty oaks.

Astronaut Al Worden said this about NASA's Apollo program, the pinnacle of American success: 'They were built by people who were nineteen feet tall for people who were nineteen feet tall, and there was a greater capacity to accept the risks of failure and loss of life in the space program in the 1960's and 1970's that doesn't fit in the culture of 2012.'

Inside each of us is that nineteen-foot tall human. Inside each of us is someone whose persistent contribution to the democratic processes of this nation can and will make a difference. You are the light that empowers someone else to take the risks, accept the challenges and help to restore the consent of the people to those whom we choose to govern.

The journey of a thousand miles begins with the first step, let this book be the inspiration, if not the guide.

CHAPTER TWO

Common Sense

On February 14th, 1776, Thomas Paine released the pamphlet *Common Sense*. At its heart, *Common Sense* sought to prove what was politically, ethically, morally, and practically wrong with English control of, and interference with, the American colonies.[1] His 'production' would prove to be the spiritual spark that lit the tinder.

It was sold and distributed widely, read aloud at taverns and meeting places. In proportion to the population of the colonies at that time (2.5 million), it had the largest sale and circulation of any book published. As of 2006, it remains the all-time best-selling American title and is still in print today.[2]

The impact it had on the citizens of the Colonies cannot be overstated. It quite literally was the very notions coalescing in the hearts and minds of these people. It provided a voice for ideas that were on the tips of tongues but could not quite be articulated. It is the absolute instance where the pen is mightier than the sword, and it truly lit the fuse for a revolution that would inspire peoples across the globe.

'The cause of America is in great measure the cause of all mankind,' wrote Thomas Paine in his introduction to *Common Sense*. His writing was in sermon form and was the first document to intellectually assert independence for the Colonies. It is precisely this style, the feel of oration, of stirring words being spoke to a crowd from a human standing on a soapbox, that gave the words such visceral and cathartic energy.

What it meant then to each citizen and the Colonies as-a-whole was to voice that which was forbidden to say: That we reserve the right to self-government by any means necessary.

As can be expected with anything revolutionary, it was met with staunch resistance. 'Perhaps the sentiments contained in the following pages, are not yet sufficiently fashionable to procure them general favor; a long habit of not thinking a thing wrong, gives it a superficial appearance of being right, and raises at first a formidable outcry in defence of custom.'[3] But then, as Thomas Paine said himself, 'Ye that oppose independence now, ye know not what you do, ye are opening the door to eternal tyranny, by keeping vacant the seat of government.'[4]

Today, as the voice of *The People* is disregarded by legislators who embrace dark money, special interests, and put their Party before their Country, Thomas Paine's words are just as relevant. Simply by replacing the words *British, monarchy, and tyrant*, with the words, *Elite, corporate, and fascist*, the present-day immediacy of *Common Sense* comes alive.

Corporations are not citizens. The consistent Supreme Court decisions to make them thus shredded the very fiber of our democracy.[5] The voice and influence of a multi-billion-dollar corporation composed of thousands of employees is not the 'citizen' our Forefathers spoke of. They would be aghast at the very notion, reaching for musket and pitchfork, taking to the streets.

In the spirit of the incendiary message that Thomas Paine used to ignite a revolution, the Constitution and the principles for which it stands, demands the same level of resistance to the Corporate Monarchy. The overthrowing of the Constitution and our Democratic Republic, the undermining of the very principle of the citizens choosing how and who will govern, is unfolding rapidly before our blinking eyes. Legislatures and corporate-sponsored entities are working against the people for their own narrow self-interests. Their bullhorn of cleverly divisive messaging divides our greatest strengths: our unity and our numbers.

It is not too late. We have before us the opportunity to save our Democratic Republic. We stand at a crossroads in America's history, at the threshold of a new age.

We must first take stock in the treasure that is America, in that which we hold dear, in the core values many have sworn to defend with their lives. We must understand in our hearts, minds, and very souls the incredible nature of The Great Experiment.

CHAPTER THREE

That Which We Hold Dear

What is it we hold dear? In a word: freedom. Freedom from, freedom for, and the inherent promise we each make that ensures freedom for all those around us.

Freedom from the destructive repression of bad government; freedom from barbarity by those outside the law; freedom from those not chosen by the people to govern, but who are enacting laws/codes/standards/practices that impair, endanger, or seek to repress the safety and happiness of all citizens; freedom from individuals/entities who influence by graft or coercion, appointed judges or elected officials.

Freedom for the opportunity to live life according to our own principles; to achieve that which we each considers successful; to have the opportunity for life, liberty, and the pursuit of happiness.

And, perhaps the most important aspect of freedom that receives such little consideration, the promise each of us makes to uphold our end. In other words, we each promise to allow everyone else the same freedoms, the same opportunities, the same access to health, wealth, and happiness. We promise to not simply *live* in this democracy, but to *participate* in it as well. Without holding ourselves accountable to this promise, democracy will slip away. The difference between democracy and oligarchy/dictatorship is the access to power and the participation in those mechanisms by the citizenry.

There is a unique symbiotic relationship between the individual and the community in a democracy. When one thinks of a fish and an anemone, there is the symbiotic relationship between an individual and the neighborhood. When one thinks of a coral reef, there is the symbiotic relationship between the neighborhood and the larger community. The scale of the metaphor can continue up to the level of the reef to the sea and the sea to the ocean. And, pivotally, from the ocean down to the individual. Engaged, happy, actualized individuals make for a vibrant, actualized environment. The reverse holds true as well, as does the axiom that the whole is only as strong as its parts.

'We hold these truths to be self-evident, that all men are created equal, that they are endowed by their creator with certain unalienable rights, that among these are Life, Liberty, and the pursuit of Happiness'.
-The Declaration of Independence

This absolutely epitomizes that which we hold dear. It is, in fact, the very foundation. Following that audacious statement is that governments are instituted by the people, and 'That whenever any Form of Government becomes destructive of these ends, it is the Right of the People to alter or abolish it.'
The inherent power of these words is what provides us with the freedom we enjoy. Not the military. Not commerce and capital. Not the corridors of power. Not the statues and monuments. These words are the cradle of democracy, the very womb from which this

great nation and other nations striving to be as free comes from. Without these words and the principles upon which they stand, this nation is nothing. The same nothing that has come before it throughout a history of nations that died like oceans polluted with malaise, corruption, greed, and anarchy.

Egypt, Persia, Rome, the many dynasties of China, the British Empire, each and every Reich, they all died from a rotten core of not allowing *all* its citizens to be free, to let the citizens be the *ones* who choose whom and how they will be governed. No matter what grandeur these empires created, their destiny was written from the first crack of slavery's whip. And in these last two paragraphs is the warning and perhaps the epithet upon the gravestone of America.

It does not need to end this way. The touchstones, the principles, the faith, hope, and charity, the core values that guided the hands writing those powerful words in the Declaration of Independence, need to be revalued and employed by each of us. If we exude these principles, then we will naturally endow them to the institutions that *we* choose to govern us.

Thucydides said, 'The secret to happiness is freedom, and the secret to freedom is courage'

It is time to revisit that which guides us. It is time to be nineteen-feet tall.

CHAPTER FOUR

That Which Guides Us

In their own words.

'And as ye would that men should do to you, do ye also to them likewise.'
-Luke 6:31

'For freedom Christ has set us free; stand firm therefore, and do not submit again to the yoke of slavery.'
-Galatians 5:1

'But let justice roll on like a river, righteousness like a never-failing stream!'
-Amos 5:24

'O mankind! We created you from a single (pair) of a male and a female, and made you into nations and tribes, that ye may know each other (not that ye may despise each other).'
-al-Hujurat # 49, v. 13

'God does not love corruption.'
-Surat al-Baqara, 205

'You cannot guide those you would like to, but God guides those He wills.'
-Holy Quran/28:56

'Thousands of candles can be lighted from a single candle, and the life of the candle will not be *s*hortened. Happiness never decreases by being shared.'
-Buddha

'With our thoughts, we make the world.'
-Buddha

'Do not be led by others, awaken your own mind, amass your own experience, and decide for yourself your own path.'
-Veda

'The secret of human freedom is to act well, without attachment to the results.'
-From the Bhagavad Gita

'This is true freedom: Our ability to shape reality. We have the power to initiate, create and change reality rather than only react and survive it. How can we all educate our children to true freedom? Teach them not to look at reality as defining their acts but to look at their acts as defining reality.'
-Yaacov Cohen

'Passover affirms the great truth that liberty is the inalienable right of every human being.'
-Morris Joseph

'When words lose their meaning, people lose their freedom.'
-Confucius

'To see the right and not do it is cowardice.'
-Confucius

'Don't you know yet? It is your light that lights the worlds.'   -Rumi

'Through discipline comes freedom.'
-Aristotle

'Who then is free? The wise man who can command himself.'
-Horace

'Common sense is both rarer and more desirable in leaders than mere intelligence.'
-Voltaire

'For in reason, all government without the consent of the governed is the very definition of slavery.'
-Jonathan Swift

'Be Americans. Let there be no sectionalism, no North, South, East or West. You are all dependent on one another and should be one in union. In one word, be a nation. Be Americans and be true to yourselves.'
-George Washington

'It is in the interest of tyrants to reduce the people to ignorance and vice. For they cannot live in any country where virtue and knowledge prevail.'
-Samuel Adams

'I grew convinced that truth, sincerity, and integrity in dealings between man and man were of the utmost importance to the felicity of life.'
-Benjamin Franklin

'We the people are the rightful masters of both Congress and the courts, not to overthrow the Constitution but to overthrow the men who pervert the Constitution.'
-Abraham Lincoln

'We must especially beware of that small group of selfish men who would clip the wings of the American Eagle in order to feather their own nests.'
-Franklin D. Roosevelt

'We the people, elect leaders not to rule but to serve.'
-Dwight D. Eisenhower

'This country cannot afford to be materially rich and spiritually poor.'
-John F. Kennedy

'Every man must decide whether he will walk in the light of creative altruism or in the darkness of destructive selfishness.'
-Martin Luther King, Jr.

'When the whole world is silent, even one voice becomes powerful.'
- Malala Yousafzai

'You can imprison a man, but not an idea. You can exile a man, but not an idea. You can kill a man, but not an idea.'
-Benazir Bhutto

If we were to embody what guides us into a precious handful of words, those words would be these: *Strength, Justice, Wisdom, Courage, Compassion, Temperance, Hope, Faith, and Charity.*

'You can blow out a candle, but you can't blow out a fire. Once the flames begin to catch, the wind will blow it higher.'
-Peter Gabriel from his song, *Biko*

CHAPTER FIVE

Uncommon Sense

With reason, we succeed. With compromise, we proceed. With common sense, we prevail.

Success is shared, whether at a personal level or as a nation. The greatest asset any business has is its people. Bottom to top, side to side, the staff governs and strives toward common goals; innovates and creates; endeavors, struggles, and overcomes.

The same is true for America. Its single greatest resource is its people, that melting pot, gumbo-stew of humanity yearning to be free. An ongoing, forever-transforming canvas being written by over three hundred million sets of hands that represent every crayon in the box. Take away one crayon, lose the art. Add crayons, enrich the art.

The success of this nation will, and has always, depended on its people. In the future, as resources will be shifted from the physical to the cerebral, the diversity, energy, and brain power of Americans as-a-whole, will determine our success.

Thus, reason. The ability to think, the ability to engage others with different ideas, and the demeanor to negotiate in good faith.

And thus, compromise. In-order to do the work of the Country, one must put the Country first. There is no other way. Byzantine, party politics, politics based not on mutual success but on the greed of a few, has always been a recipe for disaster for as long as humans have congregated together. Party politics is completely against the Constitution. It is a sure-fired way to wear that document into dust.

Duty. Honor. Country. Pretty simple stuff.

When we choose to approach the road of life in step, the struggle is much easier to endure, the chance of success that much greater. Proceeding in a Machiavellian-manner will only doom us all.

Common sense is not so common. In fact, some form of it should be taught at home, in school, and in university. Keep it simple. Keep it true. Measure twice, cut once. This works at every level and in every instance. No matter the odds, no matter the situation, common sense prevails.

'I draw my idea of the form of government from a principle in nature, which no art can overturn, viz. that the more simple any thing is, the less disordered, and the easier repaired when disordered.'[1]

Governing 330,000,000 individuals is a daunting and herculean task. By practical necessity, the instruments of governance need to be large enough to administer to this number of humans. By applying the *Common Sense* approach of Thomas Paine as stated in the quotation above, these instruments of governance should be streamlined. How then do we accomplish these contrary ideas in as seamless a way as possible?

The Republican/Libertarian mantra is that there is too much government. The Liberal/Democratic mantra is that government should provide more services. The demagogues in the media have for over a century pounded our sensibilities with derisive commentary regarding these philosophies. But what *are* the philosophies?

Democracy is defined as: *Democracy is a form of government in which the people have the authority to choose their governing legislation. Who people are and how authority is shared among them are core issues for democratic theory, development, and constitution. Some cornerstones of these issues are freedom of assembly and speech, inclusiveness and equality, membership, consent, voting, right to life and minority rights.*[2]

American Republicanism is defined as: *Republicanism is a guiding political philosophy of the United States that has been a major part of American civic thought since its founding. It stresses liberty and inalienable individual rights as central values; recognizes the sovereignty of the people as the source of all authority in law; rejects monarchy, aristocracy, and hereditary political power; expects citizens to be virtuous and faithful in their performance of civic duties; and vilifies corruption. American republican-*

ism was articulated and first practiced by the Founding Fathers in the 18th century. For them, republicanism represented more than a particular form of government. It was a way of life, a core ideology, an uncompromising commitment to liberty, and a total rejection of aristocracy.[3]

Liberalism is defined as: *Liberalism is a political and moral philosophy based on liberty, consent of the governed and equality before the law. Liberals espouse a wide array of views depending on their understanding of these principles, but they generally support free markets, free trade, limited government, individual rights, capitalism, democracy, secularism, gender equality, racial equality, internationalism, freedom of speech, freedom of the press and freedom of religion.*[4]

Libertarianism is defined as: *Libertarianism is a political philosophy and movement that upholds liberty as a core principle. Libertarians seek to maximize political freedom and autonomy, emphasizing individualism, freedom of choice and voluntary association. Libertarians share a skepticism of authority and state power.*[5]

Neoliberalism is defined as: *Neoliberalism or neo-liberalism is the 20th-century resurgence of 19th-century ideas associated with laissez-faire economic liberalism and free market capitalism, and is generally associated with policies of economic liberalization, including privatization, deregulation, globalization, free trade, austerity, and reductions in government spending in order to increase the role of the private sector in the economy and society. Neoliberalism constituted a paradigm shift away from the post-war Keynesian consensus that had lasted from 1945 to 1980.* [6]

Socialism is defined as: *Socialism is a political, social, and economic philosophy encompassing a range of economic and social systems characterized by social ownership of the means of production and workers' self-management of enterprises. It includes the political theories and movements associated with such systems. Social ownership can be public, collective, cooperative or of equity.* [7]

Setting Libertarianism, Socialism, and Neoliberalism aside, there is more in common among the three remaining, founding philosophies than there are differences. So much so, that one wonders *who and why* they have been trying so hard to divide us. *That* is the subject of the following chapter.

Cornerstones of Freedom and Liberty hallmark each of these founding philosophies. The roots of American political thought are fostered in *Common Sense*, *The Constitution*, and the *Bill of Rights*. Those inalienable rights are the primary focus of each of the core American political philosophies. The degree of participation in government, and whether that philosophy is also how one is expected to live their non-civic life, are where the differences come in.

Government created and consented by the people is where this all starts. Note, the great disdain for aristocracy and corruption in American Republicanism. Thomas Paine wrote this in Common Sense: 'That the king cannot be trusted without being looked after, or in other words, that a thirst for absolute power is the natural disease of monarchy.'[8] These words ring true through all political entities where the consent of the people on who and how they are governed is *not* the foundation or has been purchased.

Alternately, mob-rule was a very real concern among the Founding Fathers. It is why the Constitution's Article V requires that an amendment be proposed by two-thirds of the House and Senate, or by a constitutional convention called for by two-thirds of the state legislatures. And, furthermore, it is up to the states to approve a new amendment, with three-quarters of the states voting to ratifying it.

Democracy, a multi-racial democracy guaranteeing equal rights to all citizens, is the idea of the Great Experiment. This is simply the most sacred thing the Constitution upholds. Without it, in its intended form, we, as a society, slide back to the mosh pit of oligarchy and dictatorship.

Our Founding Fathers were Liberal Democrats *AND* Republicans. After nearly forty years of hate-radio and hate-television telling us we are separate, different, and enemies, this is a tough concept to wrap your heart and head around. But it is precisely so.

Yes, they argued. Yes, they were passionate. But they reasoned. Can you imagine Congress creating the Constitution today?

Yet in 1776, these struggling, passionate humans came together and gave the world our Constitution.

In recognizing the similarities of Republicanism and Liberalism, we have reasoned what unites us. Being reasonable, we will compromise some of the outlying or vague ideas so that as a nation we can proceed. And we will use common sense throughout this process to prevail in continuing the Great Experiment of American Democracy.

In our hearts, we want to believe that everyone is at least as good as ourselves. When we negotiate, we do so in the belief that the other people at the table are also there in good faith. At the very core of every human being is a desire for those Inalienable Rights, that yearning to be free, a desire to live our life the way we choose.

Naïve? Perhaps.

The higher moral ground? Undoubtedly.

Will there be those who try to exploit this good faith? Well, 'The price of Liberty is eternal vigilance'.

CHAPTER SIX

The Dark Side

'The end of democracy and the defeat of the American Revolution will occur when government falls into the hands of lending institutions and moneyed incorporations.'
-Thomas Jefferson

'The more men have to lose, the less willing they are to venture. The rich are in general slaves to fear and submit to courtly power with the trembling duplicity of a Spaniel.'
-Thomas Paine. Common Sense.

And here we are. If silence is acceptance, then vigilance has been cast aside for comfort. The consent of the people has been perverted into a way of life that demands too much for the citizens of America to have the energy and time to watch what has been happening in the shadows. A powerplay by vain and aspiring men to usurp this democracy in favor of a system of government that empowers and enriches the few at the expense of the many.

Dark Money is political spending by nonprofit organizations that are not required to disclose their donors. Such entities can receive unlimited donations from corporations, individuals, and other organizations. This allows those donating influence on elections and other political functions with complete anonymity. Spending of this nature went from 5.2 million in 2006, to over 300 million in 2012. The Supreme Court decision in 2010 in Citizens United vs. FEC literally opened the floodgates.[1]

The use of Dark Money to tilt the courts; to bankroll the campaigns of legislators; to create bogus entities with misleading names to trick the citizenry into thinking that they are defending their freedoms; to form think tanks and institutes that purport to be fact/science-based to sway the public away from actual objective scientific facts that would stand in the way of profits; these men and their Dark Money are the chief enemy of the United States.

In addition to this, and at some level coupled right along with it, are a bankrolled populist media that acts as an amplifier of disinformation for the sources of all this corruption. Divide and conquer. The simple fact that every working man and woman in this country, regardless of ideology/philosophy/background, has more in common with each other than the trust fund children of the Corporate Monarchy is conveniently brushed aside by appealing to xenophobia, race-baiting, toxic masculinity, and the conjured-up culture wars through the populist media.

With the advent of social media, (a force multiplier for the caustic, divisive populist media), the derision shown to education, the scorn shown to science, an all-too-easily manipulated electorate regarding abortion and the Second Amendment, a populace that is more willing to believe propaganda than facts, and you can see the poisonous stew the Great Melting Pot has become.

Lest the United States becomes a corporate version of the current Chinese government, or the Christian Republic of America, a red, white, and blue version of Iran, we will roll our sleeves up, set our jaws with grim determination, put aside the bombastic rants of ideologues, and examine each of these threats to our Democratic Republic.

Dark Money is the single greatest threat to democracy. Dark Money is an endless slush fund for judicial candidates, legislative candidates, political action committees, trade associations, and 'think tanks.' The principal financiers of this Dark Money have so tilted the legislative and judicial playing fields, have so distorted the information reaching the public, and have so divided American society, that it will take years to unravel the mess.

The Republican Party, the bastion of conservative thought, has been reduced to a party of the special interests of a small handful of vain and aspiring men. It no longer represents its constituents, increasingly casting aside the will of the people for the direction of its financial backers. The very existence of the Republican Party as a viable entity in this democracy is in question, unless of course there is no longer a democracy.

'Although nobody agrees with me, I am of the opinion that the only sound countries in the world are Germany, Italy and Japan, simply because they are all working and working hard.'
-Fred Chase Koch. American. 1938.[2]

In 1934, William Rhodes Davis, an American Nazi sympathizer with extensive business dealings in the Third Reich, teamed with Fred Koch to build a refinery in Hamburg capable of processing a thousand tons of crude oil into high octane fuel. It was finally destroyed by Allied bombing on June 18th, 1944. Which means, that the Allied troops landing at Normandy on June 6th, 1944, were being engaged by an enemy powered by Fred Koch's gasoline. He is, after all, the man who came up with a better process to turn oil into gasoline and aviation fuel, and then sold it to the Nazis.

In 1958, Fred Koch started The John Birch Society. Once a fringe element in American politics, so much so that even William F. Buckley and The National Review denounced it, 'Bircherism' has sprung back to become the central core of beliefs in the "conservative" philosophy.[3] That much of their rhetoric is based on conspiracy theory seems to not matter a wit, science and facts have no place in this sphere of politics.

Charles and David Koch, Fred's sons, are two of the wealthiest individuals on the planet. Their wealth comes from the refining of oil into gasoline and chemicals. Massive investments of this money have further increased their wealth. Tacking alongside this entrepreneurial spirit is a deep belief in limited government, personal freedom, and a deregulated free-enterprise system. On the surface, this libertarian/neoliberalist view would seem not too far removed from our Founding Father's beliefs. However, at the same time, these two people have invested hundreds of millions of dollars to do exactly what are Founding Fathers warned us about.

In 1980, David ran for Vice-President as a Libertarian. The basic platform was to do away with all government programs, including taxes, and privatize all aspects of society. They were trounced. Undaunted, he and his brother began a more insidious way to incorporate these narrow ideas into mainstream society.

Already responsible for busting up unions in the Koch plants and funding legislation to weaken them further, they began to wreak further havoc on the fabric of American society. Besides massive clandestine pollution at their plants, they funded university research institutes, think tanks, and industry trade associations that would propagate and publish misinformation about climate change and government social programs.

From 1998 to 2008, their spending on lobbying increased from hundreds of thousands to many millions in their attempts to squelch climate change measures being considered by Congress. They funded the Tea Party and were instrumental in eliminating every moderate Republican from Congress.

Some of the think tanks and organizations the Koch's have funded are State Policy Network, Heartland Institute, Manhattan Institute for Policy Research, Texas Public Policy Foundation, Pacific Research Institute, Independent Women's Forum, Fraser Institute, George C. Marshall Institute, Capital Research Center, Cato Institute, Federalist

Society, Mercatus Center, Institute for Humane Studies, Institute for Justice, Heritage Foundation, Institute for Energy Research, American Enterprise Institute, Foundation for Accountability and Civic Trust, Aspen Institute, FreedomWorks, Americans for Prosperity, and Citizens for the Environment.

Articles written under the auspices of one of the above were distributed to news outlets as real news. Many newspapers, magazines, internet news sites, talk radio broadcasters, and television news broadcasts are duped into carrying fake news because it comes from some important sounding "think tank".[3]

This article in *Medium* encapsulates the deep research in Jane Mayer's *Dark Money*, and *Kochland*, by Christopher Leonard.

The philosophy at the core of their beliefs is neoliberalism. It is a direct, pendulum-swinging reaction to the Keynesian-economic model adopted by most countries in the early part of the 20th Century. The Keynes model was itself a direct, pendulum-swinging reaction to the abhorrent social/working conditions and economic disparity resulting from the Industrial Revolution. A hands-off approach to economics, *Laissez-Faire*, was the policy that had created the environment that sparked revolutions around the world.

Enter John Maynard Keynes, who believed in balancing the playing field between the haves and the have-nots by taxing the haves and creating government-controlled safety nets. This was naturally opposed by the 'haves', who saw such a response as a power-grab for their property/prosperity. Important to note, that socialism also rose-up at this time in response to the abject situation that most people faced.

Since the end of World War Two, an increasingly louder voice of Neoliberalism was surfacing. Guided by the Austrian School, an economic theory that went so far as to claim itself as an applied science, Fred Koch and other wealthy individuals began to adopt the principles of the Austrian School, and to fund/influence its application/education.

Neoliberalist economics is a return to the beginning of the Industrial Revolution. Neoliberalism fails to account for the most important aspect of economics: that economics exists only as a facility for the interaction of human beings. And wherever there are human beings, there is going to be an exponent shaped like a question mark mucking-up the whole equation.

Humans, and therefore Ethics, are where most scientific approaches to economics go off the rails. It is one thing to observe, report and create theory; it is an entirely different thing to take theory and create applications. You cannot measure theory.

In pure capitalism, there is little intrinsic value for doing the right thing, for putting community above self, for not stepping on everyone around you. Pure capitalism does not temper the worst parts of human nature.

Think of it this way: How does the boardgame *Monopoly* end? Yup. With one fat cat and everyone else broke.

How better to achieve that Monopoly-end game than with Dark Money. Along with property, why not own the legislators, own the judges, own the political party to which they belong, own unsuspected sources of disinformation, and then rake in unfettered profits from your fossil fuel companies. Why even pay taxes? Might as well tilt that field as well.

How did this happen?

A perfect storm of policies, laws, societal changes brought on largely by technology, and a cadre of wealthy neoliberalists working this storm to their advantage. The Koch's are one of a dozen tribes and industries attempting a decades-long larceny of America, a theft that continues by inches, squeezing the middle class into non-existence, and creating levels of poverty not seen since the Industrial Revolution.

Understanding the methodology of the Koch's leads to an understanding of how we got to this point in American history. It also points to where this level of influence is headed, particularly since the Supreme Court's decision in *Citizens United vs. Federal Election Commission* opened the nation's elections to obscene amounts of Dark Money.

This leads to Robert and Rebekah Mercer, Robert Herring, Rupert Murdoch, and the intertwining of Dark Money, nationalism, populism, racism, and social media. The outsized influence of these individuals and their billions of dollars to the fabric of American society is being played out as these words are written. Mr. Mercer has been quoted as saying that the 1964 Civil Rights Act was the worst thing to happen to the country. He and his daughter's funding of Breitbart, Parler[5], and numerous entities/individuals with equally racist, nationalistic, and conspiracy theory-based agendas, has coalesced a deluded, violent, and fascist counter current. Robert Herring is responsible for One America News, and Mr. Murdoch is the creator of Fox News, pages torn from Soviet-style television which habitually flouts truth, and is essentially propaganda. Where once the fringe of the extreme right was both morally and financially bankrupt, it now enjoys center stage and robust funding.

The siege on the Capital building on January 6th, 2021? Thank the Mercer's, Mr. Herring, Mr. Murdoch, and an host of equally mendacious individuals. Also thank a Republican party that forgot country comes before party; that forgot what it means to be conservative; and that allowed themselves to be bought.

Two quotes from President Dwight D. Eisenhower:

'If a political party does not have its foundation in the determination to advance a cause that is right and that is moral, then it is not a political party; it is merely a conspiracy to seize power.'

'A people that values its privileges above its principles soon loses both.'

Two recent instances that prove the mendacity, insidiousness, and complete disregard for democracy of what once was the Party of Lincoln:

REDMAP (short for Redistricting Majority Project) is a project of the Republican State Leadership Committee of the United States to increase Republican control of Congressional seats as well as state legislators, largely through determination of electoral district boundaries. The project has reportedly made effective use of partisan gerrymandering, by relying on previously unavailable mapping software such as *Maptitude* to improve the precision with which district lines are strategically drawn. The strategy was focused on swing blue states like Pennsylvania, Ohio, Michigan, North Carolina, and Wisconsin where there was a Democratic majority but which they could swing towards Republican with appropriate redistricting. The project was launched in 2010 and estimated to have cost the Republican party around US$30 million.[6]

Texas v. Pennsylvania, 592 U.S. (2020), was a lawsuit filed at the United States Supreme Court contesting the administration of the 2020 presidential election in certain states, in which Joe Biden defeated incumbent Donald Trump.

Filed by Texas Attorney General Ken Paxton on December 8, 2020, under the Supreme Court's original jurisdiction, Texas v. Pennsylvania alleged that Georgia, Michigan, Pennsylvania, and Wisconsin violated the United States Constitution by changing election procedures through non-legislative means. The suit sought to temporarily withhold the certified vote count from these four states prior to the Electoral College vote on December 14. The suit was filed after about 50 lawsuits arising from disputes over the election results filed by Trump and the Republican Party had failed in numerous state and federal courts.

Within one day of Texas's filing, Trump, over 100 Republican Representatives, and 18 Republican state attorney generals filed motions to support the case. The incumbent president referred to this case as "the big one". Attorneys general for the defendant states, joined in briefs submitted by their counterparts from twenty other states, two territories, and the District of Columbia, urged the Court to refuse the case, calling it a "seditious abuse of the judicial process." Legal experts argued that the case was not likely to be heard and not likely to succeed if it got heard, and thus it was a "Hail Mary" action.

The Supreme Court issued orders on December 11, declining to hear the case on the basis that Texas lacked standing under Article III of the Constitution to challenge the results of the election held by another state.[7]

When confronted by competition, there are two different strategies that can be employed: one can either improve their product, sharpen their message, revitalize their skill set, in-other-words, get better; or they can cheat.

A wise man once told his son, as his son was about to leave for his first important gig as a successful musician, 'Now, you have a microphone, and with that microphone comes a responsibility'.

Hitler had a microphone. He even had a minion to run that microphone, Paul Joseph Goebbels, Reich Minister of Propaganda. They understood the reach, the power, the ability to sway an entire populace with the magic of this new technology called radio. They understood that by telling people the same thing over and over, regardless of its truth, regardless of whether it was morally justified, regardless of who it could hurt, that after a time enough people would believe it. For the Nazis, the 'stab-in-the-back myth' became a central tenet in the Nazi message to the German people.

From then until now, the allure and magic of the microphone has been amplified by television, the internet, smart phones, and social media. From then until now, the world has had the misfortune to have had dozens of Hitlers and thousands of Goebbels barking their diatribe into their microphones. And from then until now, just enough people have believed that diatribe to make the world a dangerous and divided place.

In America, for over sixty years, and with roots going back even further, the central tenets of the message to be hammered home are that liberals will take away your civil liberties, that liberals are in fact socialists, that government cannot be trusted, and that pure capitalism will solve all social issues. The simple fact that all of us lives in a Liberal Democracy created by Republican Revolutionaries, was never mentioned. Obviously, the people with the microphone hammering these messages are those who stand to profit the most from these messages.

Today, the microphone is completely out of control. The caustic divide in America is largely caused by divisive diatribe from the populist media. Their microphone is being financed by people who are refusing compromise, blocking progress, and tearing down the fabric of society. This is something on a different order from previous fringe movements in America. This is powered by Dark Money and uber-amplified. This is a harbinger for impending autocracy.

The Media, in all its warty, imposing, intrusive, gigantic ugliness, has reached a level of pervasiveness that Emile Berliner, the inventor of the microphone, could hardly have imagined. Truth is no longer stranger than fiction because truth has been relegated to a backseat role. In a country that prides itself on rugged individualism, few individuals take the time to ascertain the "information" that is *posed* in front of them. And then, with one click, send the garbage to more individuals who are likely to be just as flippant.

An entire chapter in this book is dedicated to *The Media*. The microphone has been replaced by *'info-tainment'*. It is important to remember two things: one, nearly all News/Information distribution is corporate-owned and therefore a slave to profit; and two, it is increasingly populist. Neither of these two points will let truth get in the way.

In understanding the corporate nature of *The Media*, it doesn't take too much of a jump, or any degree of rugged individualism, to make the connection between Dark Money and the Populist Media. In fact, if Hitler and Goebbels had Twitter, Facebook, You Tube, Alt-Television, and the rest of the panoply, nary a shot need have been fired to conquer all of Europe. A fact that several Foreign Intelligence Services know all too well.

Government is not the problem. Corrupt government is the problem. The people/entities that are trying to convince America that government is the problem, are the people/entities corrupting the government. The tools they are using to do so are Dark Money, Populist and Divisive Media, Political Action Committees/Lobbying, and gerrymandering/voter repression. Effective communication and education of who these people/entities are, which judges/legislators have been financed by them, and what tools we the people can use to counter this attack on our democracy is the beginning of a solution.

The Defense Industry, the Fossil Fuel Industry, the Insurance Industry, the Pharmaceutical Industry, The Media, and the principal banks that finance much of these industries, are largely owned by a small number of men. These men, hiding behind corporate boards, engage in a Byzantine game of power and wealth. Tilting the field to their own individual advantages, no matter the cost to the greater good, is no more to them than lighting a cigarette. The word to describe such disregard for anyone other than themselves is sociopath.

'Permit me to issue and control the money of a nation, and I care not who makes its laws!'

This oft cited quote rings prophetically true. Follow the wealth discussed in this chapter and you will always end up in the corridors of power. Follow this money and you will find an agenda laced with greed and hiding behind The Constitution and civil liberties.

Their greed is also their Achilles heel. Renewed stringent regulation on the banks, Campaign Finance Reform with complete transparency, spending caps, digitally recorded meetings in public spaces between lobbyists and politicians, a refinement of the process of legislation, eliminating the electoral college and the filibuster, a set, finite timetable for elections, and renewing the Fairness Doctrine, solves much of this in one fell swoop.

This is no conspiracy theory. There are no assumptions. The above statements are factual and can be easily researched. There exists a body of work substantiating the claims. There is a paper trail that can be followed. The aforementioned-authors, numerous dissertations, studies, books, articles, news programs, and this author have arrived at these conclusions by using the four greatest tools available for detective work: deductive reasoning, inductive reasoning, Occam's Razor, and *follow-the-money*.

The end-result of these machinations by this new Ruling Class will be a one-party, oligarchical republic where elections are as faux as they are in China, Russia, Iran, or North Korea. The not-too-distant horizon from this oligarchical republic is an entity that has a State Party, a State Religion, and the end of all civil liberties. History is replete with examples of this happening. Absolute power corrupts absolutely.

Is it too late for us to turn the tide?

No.

The Human Spirit instinctively produces the desire to be free. It also produces courage.

Are humans simply too conditioned and too lazy to avoid powerplays of this nature?

Hell no.

There is the shot heard 'round the world.

There is the image of one fellow with a briefcase standing in front of a tank.

And there are 330,000,000 of us yearning to be free.

CHAPTER SEVEN

Better Angels

'When we lose the right to be different, we lose the privilege to be free.'
-Charles Evans Hughes

Aren't we blessed to have such diverse and passionate political beliefs!

Aren't we blessed to have Progressives on the left, brainstorming ideas and visions for the future.

Aren't we blessed to have Conservatives on the right, studying how those ideas and visions might work for the Nation.

Aren't we blessed to have Moderates in the middle asking the Progressives and the Conservatives to pull together so we can all move forward with the business of the Country.

Patriotism isn't about tearing America apart it's about building America up. Patriotism is not about more government or less government, it's about better government, government that listens to the voices of all its citizens. Patriotism isn't about minutemen, militias, and violence, it's about participation, people, and perseverance. This Nation may at times be dysfunctional, but its far from being broken. And anyone telling you it is broken, is selling you snake oil.

That tension between the left and right is the lifeblood of the Nation. Where the opposites in a culture clash, that's where the real progress is being made. Without that energy the heartbeat of the Nation stops. That is why autocracies always perish: a one-sided relationship can never survive.

It is so important as Americans to understand that without the opposing views of fellow Americans, without reasonable debate of ideas and issues, the very life of this democracy ceases. Patriotism is not a competition. Liberty is not about winning. The essence of freedom is in allowing everyone to be free.

'We make a living by what we get, but we make a life by what we give.'
-Winston Churchill

We each make *The Promise* when we proclaim ourselves as Americans, when we embrace the liberty and freedom that makes this nation so great. We promise to let all of those around us have life, liberty, and to pursue happiness. A quote from Supreme Court Justice Oliver Wendell Holmes, Jr. says it all: 'The right to swing my fist ends where the other man's nose begins.'

An excellent example of this is smoking in public. The individual's right to smoke was forced to give way to the rights of those who do not wish to inhale the second-hand smoke. Now ultimately, the celebrity death match that probably forced the hand on this issue was the insurance industry taking the tobacco industry to the mat, but in essence the dictum is sound: one's right to smoke infringes on another's right to breathe.

This also highlights an integral part of *The Promise*: Personal Responsibility. That cornerstone of conservative philosophy goes hand-in-glove with Personal Freedom. The respect we afford those around us is circular.

We give it and expect to receive it. That process extends to more than physical space. It also extends to where people come from, how they look, what they believe, whom they love, and how they choose to live. Live and let live takes freedom to another level.

We also promise to contribute more than simply punching a clock, paying our bills, and paying taxes. We promise to participate in the democratic process. Without our participation, without our vigilance, people/entities like those mentioned in the previous chapter can work their corruption. Slippage occurs when we fail to pay attention.

We also promise to be a part of the community. To give back. To empower. To help-out and help up. The altruistic nature of Americans is well known with an estimated two-thirds of us giving to charity, ranking the U.S. fourth in the world.[1]

It is easy to forget these promises. It is easy to forget that there is more to life than personal freedom, than acquiring, than being in it only for ourselves. The nature of freedom is to work at maintaining that freedom. Not an easy task when faced with the demands of the day. The simple fact that wages haven't kept pace with growth[2] has forced families to hold down multiple jobs, further complicating the precious few minutes in an overloaded day. It is easy to only see the tree for the forest, to be overwhelmed by day-to-day survival.

That is the shadow. The light is the strength of each of us to not just endure against these odds, but to make our families, our neighborhoods, and our communities robust, actualized, wonderful places that thrive.

Prudence. Justice. Temperance. Fortitude. Faith. Hope. Charity. When we make the promise to America to be an American, these seven codes of conduct combine to be our pole star. We expect it from those we elect, we expect it from those we do business with, and ultimately, we expect it from ourselves. It takes great courage to demand this of one's self. It takes great effort to work toward embodying these principles. Yet, somewhere deep inside us is an innate desire to be all of this and much more. *A desire to be the pole star itself.* In the sense that the light we emanate empowers those around us to shine as well. Imagine a nation that quite literally glows with the light of its people.

That is why no one gets left behind. Franklin Delano Roosevelt spoke of four freedoms: freedom of speech; freedom of worship; freedom from fear; freedom from want. If as a nation we worked to achieve these four most basic human needs, we would elevate America to a level unknown in the history of human beings. The means, the sheer capital to achieve this already exists. It is up to us as citizens to demand from our elected officials, from our institutions, and from ourselves, a reprioritizing of what is important, and the allocation of resources to achieve those ends.

Imagine a nation where every person has an equal opportunity. Where every person has the same starting point. Where the basic, necessities of life are available, just in case. Where *all* school systems no longer worry about funding. Where a college education isn't just a dream, but a reality, and a reality where economic slavery to debt isn't the end result. The resources already exist to do this. And to be perfectly frank, this can all be done with a combined effort of government, the private sector, and non-profit organizations. And furthermore, it can be done with long term national success and short-term profit at every step along the way.

The songs that define America, the *National Anthem*, *America The Beautiful*, *My Country Tis of Thee*, are stirring, beautiful, patriotic songs. Let us add a song to that pantheon that has no words, yet lifts the heart and soul, emboldens, and imbues courage: Aaron Copland's *Fanfare For The Common Man*. Inspired by the words of Vice President Henry A. Wallace in 1942, when Wallace proclaimed the dawning of the "century of the common man", the power and essence of this piece is what embodies Americans. Where words can be bungled, burgled, and baffling, the power of Copland's *Fanfare* is that it reaches each listener individually, allowing that person to etch their own words on their own heart. This *is* the American spirit.

Peace and prosperity. What we hope for. What we strive for. The apple pie that is the American economy is the largest and most diverse economy in the history of the world. It is so immense and vibrant the sucker punch that was the Great Recession of 2008 could not bring the Country to its knees. A blow that would have felled empires, America staggered, wiped the blood from the corner of its mouth, and then rolled-up its sleeves. In this immense economy, there is enough resources to provide the Common Man with everything mentioned above. In other words, a common starting point for each person; an infrastructure that streamlines communication, commerce, and transportation; a nation that invests in its people, in science, in the fabric of society. All of this while still protecting its citizens at every level. This is more than possible. It simply requires taking the means of slicing the apple pie away from the monied corporations and returning it to the people.

Lest the monied corporations forget, without the Common Man they are nothing. In peace and prosperity, in a country as imagined above, the American apple pie economy grows many, many times larger, enriching everyone.

One of the first places to start is addressing the National Minimum Wage. A 2021 study by the Congressional Budget Office[3] states that raising the minimum wage to $15 an hour by 2025 would result in pulling 900,000 out of poverty, raise wages for nearly 27 million Americans, and create a loss of 1.4 million jobs. What this study does not take-into-account is what that extra income could provide, and where that extra income would go. In other words, these new middle-class people would be spending, saving, and potentially opening businesses, all of which would replace the jobs lost.

A comprehensive article in *Journalist's Resource*[4] used information from government and academic studies that showed largely positives, that the negatives were never as severe as advertised, and that tax revenues at all levels were greatly increased. It showed that many states, cities, and large corporations throughout the nation have already implemented a $15 minimum wage with little or no effect regarding jobs lost.

The effect that a gradual increase in minimum wage has on small businesses is the issue that gains the most traction with those who are content with the status quo. The actual answer to this nebulous question is that an economy is only as strong as its middle class. Yes, there will be casualties in the short term, as there always is with societal change. No, it will not be catastrophic. In fact, the extra buying power of 27 million people will cushion most of the short-term pain.

The upstream economic gains of this cannot be scoffed at or ignored: more tax revenue, less government spending on poverty, less crime, the tremendous addition of monies across the economic spectrum. Those positives are just in the first decade. Imagine the effect this added purchasing power does for the future: 401k's, savings accounts, college tuition, new homes. In a word, jobs.

To quote Nelson Mandela, 'A Nation should not be judged by how it treats its highest citizens, but it's lowest ones.' The people clinging to the status quo are unable to fathom industry without a cheap labor force. This philosophy will soon embrace robotics and artificial intelligence, thereby creating another inflection point where workers will need to be retrained. The immoral imperative inherent in the exploitation of human beings is being confronted daily around the world. How then will American society treat its citizens when this next wave of technology inevitably sweeps the jobs scape? We currently live in a country where, according to the National Low Income Housing Coalition's annual "Out of Reach" report, a person making minimum wage cannot afford a one-bedroom apartment in 95% of the counties in the United States. Obviously, something needs to be done. Wages need to be raised;

opportunities need to be afforded. An entire class of hungry, homeless citizens will break the bank, and perhaps the Democratic Republic, if the minimum wage is not raised.

One of the greatest springboards to the success of America in the Twentieth Century was the G.I. Bill. When the soldiers, sailors, and airmen returned from defeating fascism after World War II, 7.8 million of them by 1956 had used the G.I. Bill for college or a vocational training program. Historians and economists judge the G.I. Bill as a major economic success. It must have worked, as it's been resurrected many times since then[5].

Without the Cognitive Revolution, homo sapiens would quite likely have been eaten into extinction. The greatest asset we have is our ability to think. Throughout history, the nurturing of that ability has proven pivotal to our continued success.

Education opens doors for both the individual and the society. Logic dictates that the greater the access to education for the society, the greater the rewards the society reaps. Education is insurance paying forward for the future existence of the society. The benefits of education in the short term are a skilled workforce. The benefits of education in the long term are the progress of the society itself in all aspects of the human endeavor.

Education comes with a price. It has become a price that most Americans can no longer afford. While the rest of the world understands the benefits of educating its citizens, education in America has become an increasingly difficult proposition. A proposition that results in substantial debt, thereby handcuffing generations of Americans.

This is a negative on many levels. It limits the quality and quantity of new workers. It stagnates the economy by limiting the access to society of the new worker. It diminishes the prospects of these new workers. It discourages young people from seeking education. It makes America less competitive in the global marketplace. It limits possibilities for the future. It narrows the scope of the human endeavor.

The limitless potential of every human being is essentially what America is all about. By creating an education system that only favors the affluent, the American Dream becomes a money maze, a trap. The short-sightedness of pursuing the current course of education in America, at every level, is a recipe for disaster. The limitless potential of every American inside an education system that is fully engaged for them, creates an environment in which there are no problems, only solutions. Every single issue facing this nation becomes solvable.

The money it costs to properly educate every child through 2-years of college/vocational training will pay for itself in short order. The recipe for success is this: investment in fully funded schools where the money makes it to the student; students, teachers, and administrators being held to high levels of excellence; and government from local to federal making it a priority to educate each American. This combination of goals will create an economy the likes of which has never been seen before.

Where bureaucracies stifle progress, trim the fat. Where funding is short, provide the funds. Where teachers are lacking, make those jobs irresistible. At the end of the day, we may laud superstar athletes and pop stars, but it's the educators who actually inspire. It is educators that hold the key for the success of America.

The average salary for an American with a two-year degree is over $41,000. The unemployment rate is 3.8%

The average salary for an American without a High School diploma is $25,000. The unemployment rate is 8%[6].

The economic benefits of education are undeniably important to the U.S. In the country alone, GDP has potential to increase by $32 trillion, or 14.6 percent if all students are brought up to basic mastery by the National Assessment of Educational Progress standards. Intensive efforts at test score maximization for students in a handful of states with highest economic performance in the U.S. can increase GDP by $76 trillion over approaching decades. Furthermore, improvements in education according to spending on K-12 schooling is said to reap more improvements from investment than the burden of the cost.[7]

The *Return on Investment* of education is greater than any other public or private investment. As the loss of manufacturing jobs to automation, consolidation, and outsourcing created a sense of disenfranchisement among two generations of Rustbelt Americans, the opportunity to retrain these individuals and communities came and went unaddressed. Many saw the writing on the wall, pulled themselves up by their bootstraps and developed new skill sets. Many more did not, could not, and were never acknowledged. Imagine if this had been approached differently. Imagine if these people had been retrained. It has been forty-plus years since the manufacturing jobs started drying up, the *Return on Investment* of these millions of people would have erased a large portion of the National Debt.

The third fetter holding America back is Health Care. The cost of Health Care services, premiums, and deductibles is crushing the American Middle Class. It doesn't even exist for the lower classes, which creates a debt-feedback loop that strangles the society. America is the only very highly developed nation to not have Universal Health Care.[8]

Why is this? Here's a brief summation:

Ultimately, the United States remains one of the only advanced industrialized nations without a comprehensive national health in-

surance system and with little prospect for one developing under the next president because of the many ways America is exceptional.

Its culture is unusually individualistic, favoring personal over government responsibility; lobbyists are particularly active, spending billions to ensure that private insurers maintain their status in the health system; and our institutions are designed in a manner that limits major social policy changes from happening. As long as these facts remain, there is little reason to expect universal coverage in America anytime soon, regardless of who becomes president.[9]

Those words were written in 2016. A CBS News poll taken three years later showed that 66% of Americans now favor a governmental health plan for all. What changed? Well, in 1960 the average annual per person cost of health care was $147. In 2018 it rose to $11,172. Health Care costs have risen faster than the median annual income.[10]

No matter how much money is lobbied against Universal Health Care from special interests, no matter how many lies are spewed from pulpits and pundits, no matter how difficult the obstacle course of governmental inertia to formally address the issue, the simple fact is that a substantial majority of Americans cannot afford health care. Americans who vote. Americans who would love to be larger participants in the economy. Americans whose American Dream is flat lining.

This is an exceptionally complicated issue. There is, however, already a system in place in Australia that would work quite well. A two-tier health care system that has at its foundation Medicare, coupled with Private Health Insurance. This system has effectively halved the percent of GDP that is paid into health care, the per capita, and the infant mortality rate as compared to the United States. Much of the core of this system already exists in the U.S. What is lacking is removing Special Interests from destroying any effort of solving the issue; and getting accurate information to the American public.[11]

This is not Socialized Medicine. Every American chooses what level of care is best for them and their families, or if they want it at all. It decreases costs without effecting the level of care. It removes the burden of health care costs from businesses making them more competitive, unless of course they still want to offer Health Care as an incentive.

Health Care is not a privilege. It is a fundamental right. The protection, welfare, and care of one's people is the primary responsibility of government. If one does not have their health, they have nothing. Healthy people equal a healthy economy. 66% of Americans are in favor of some form of National Health Care.[12] The Covid-19 Pandemic illustrated with deadly accuracy how inept a for-profit health care industry is. There are areas of life where government has no right to interfere, and there are areas of life where some level of cohesion, organization, and policing is necessary. This is one of the areas where a shepherd is needed to guard the flock.

If America were to adequately address these three issues alone, the nation would sincerely be that shining city on the hill. The better angels of our nature's demands that something be done to address the widening gap between the wealthiest and the poorest. History shows all too well the inevitable result of a shrinking middle class, of a nation where the many are being crushed by the few.

And as such, we come to that most uncomfortable conversation: The Safety Net.

Come, you who are blessed by my Father, inherit the kingdom prepared for you from the foundation of the world. For I was hungry and you gave me food, I was thirsty and you gave me drink, I was a stranger and you welcomed me, I was naked and you clothed me, I was sick and you visited me, I was in prison and you came to me.
-Matthew 25: 34-36

Fish? Or teach to fish? In practical terms, a nation needs to do both. Feed the person. Take care of those basic human necessities. Then teach them how to do so on their own.

There is no 'one-size fits all' with this. People learn differently and with varying speeds. The important thing as a society is to give the less fortunate the opportunity. As in education, some students learn quickly and rise swiftly; others struggle and lag; and there are those few who seem unable or unwilling to learn at all. The decisions in charity, as in most of society, needs to come from the ground up. The 'boots-on-the-ground' are in the best position to gauge where each person is at in this process.

Now, in saying this, there isn't a never-ending public pool of resources to be taken advantage of. At the same time, the number of people jacking the system has been completely blown out of proportion by elements of *Movement Conservatism/neoliberalism*.[13] Given forty years of uncontrolled diatribe, (as described in *The Dark Side* chapter and again in the *Capital Radio* chapter), the image of Welfare Queens, as espoused by President Reagan, has taken on a life of its own, largely devoid of evidence.

The numbers on Welfare are ridiculously skewed depending on the source. The simplest way to get actual data is to go to the Federal Budget for that year. In 2019, about 10.5% of the population was living in poverty, roughly 35 million people. This is half of what it was coming out of the Great Recession.[14] The federal government spent 773 billion on Medicaid, SNAP, and other safety net programs in 2019.[15] On the surface this is like spending $20,000 per person. The Federal Poverty Line for 2019 was just under $12,500.

So, what to do?

From a Common Sense, economic perspective, the best solution is to take care of the poor in the short term, train these folks, and then get them on their feet and on their own. Their being valid parts of the economy repays whatever resources were needed in the short term.

From a straight budget-hawk perspective, the amount of money being spent on defense, corporate subsidies, and foreign aid to first-world countries, would prove to have more impact on balancing the budget. The need for oversight and streamlining are crucial in any bureaucracy, and since *The Safety Net* has become the principal target for folks deathly afraid of government overreach, it is even more crucial to run these departments with complete transparency.

The *Better Angels of Our Natures* response is already clarified by the words from the Gospel According to Matthew. In essence, there really is no other response. One simply can't have Christ in one hand and the budget in the other. If a society can't help its own people, then it has failed its chief responsibility. This can, however, be done efficiently. One cannot deposit Hope, Faith, and Charity into one's bank account, but what those three virtues create can move mountains.

The other side of the coin is what is the cost of doing nothing? Crime? Death? Chaos? Urban blight? All the possible scenarios of doing less cost society even more.

Poverty is eliminated with opportunity. The numbers show that after the Great Recession poverty in America spiked. Since then, as opportunities rebounded with the economy, poverty abated. The driving force behind this is that people do not want to be poor. They will seek out opportunities.

Fish, *and* teach to fish, understanding that there is a higher law than the Constitution, than balanced budgets, than legislation.

Now, had wages kept pace with growth since 1968, the issues mentioned above are moot. If the National Minimum Wage had kept pace with Productivity Growth since 1968, the minimum wage would be $24 an hour. A person making minimum wage working a forty-hour work week would make $48,000 a year.[16] Suddenly, Health Care, College, Home Ownership, in a nutshell, The

American Dream, becomes a reality. Suddenly poverty, crime, and the burden on The Safety Net, becomes much less.

As it stands, the Minimum Wage has not kept pace with inflation, much less Productivity Growth. We are, society-wise, GDP-wise, and Government Revenue-wise, living with the consequences. Would the additional costs of labor make American products less competitive? Yes, and no. There would really be no reason for business or government to provide health care or pensions. Productivity would be higher due to incentive. The skill-level of the American worker would be higher due to education. The drag on the economy from social poverty would be less. More than all that, the spending capability of your average American would be greatly enhanced, thus infusing the economy with tremendous amounts of money.

Some interesting notes from 1979 to 2019: the percentage of the GDP being spent on Social Security and Medicare has gone up less than 4%; the percentage of GDP of Medicaid and other Safety Net programs has increased by less than 4%; the share of wealth by the top 1% has gone up by over 17%; the number of workers in Unions has decreased by nearly 40%; the percentage of income tax as part of the GDP is roughly the same[17]; all while the United States has added over 100 million citizens. In 2019, 60 million people on average a month received welfare of some kind. Two more things: the number of people in poverty is 8 million more than it was in 1979[18]; and the Real GDP went from 6.8 trillion (1979) to 19 trillion (2019)[19].

What does this tell us? Quite simple, the money does not trickle down. Despite the Better Angels of Our Natures, it takes shepherds in the guise of laws, regulations, watch dogs, the Safety Net, and Unions to protect the flock. Common Sense and logic would not dictate otherwise. What demonstrates the need for vigilance in stark relief is how Neo-liberalists are trying to convince the public that Social Security and Medicare are entitlements, despite each of us paying into those funds with every check.

'We hold these truths to be self-evident, that all men are created equal, that they are endowed, by their Creator, with certain unalienable Rights, that among these are Life, Liberty, and the pursuit of Happiness.'
-Thomas Jefferson

The population of America has increased 130 times the population in 1776. Each one of the now 330,000,000 Americans deserves what Thomas Jefferson so eloquently wrote; and each of those Americans likewise makes *The Promise* to each other and the Country. It is in the complexity of that equation, that wonderful limbo between "I" and "We", where we discover our "American-ness". Because quite simply, at a fundamental level, we are truly in this together. E Pluribus Unum: From Many, One.

The breadth and depth of Americans, the incredible array of skill sets, knowledge, talents, and experience, is unmatched in the history of this species. The tools of education, economy, and resources, driven by a people whose energy has no limits, can not only solve monumental problems, but create entire futures.

What we can achieve together dwarfs any juvenile fantasies of ideologues or demagogues. Those who try to divide us, who try to tear down this egalitarian Democratic Republic, who seek through pulpit and pundit to crush the common man, can never win. History once more is replete with the human spirit rising above all odds.

America did not appear in a vacuum, or out of thin air, or by happenstance. Human Beings have been yearning for this. Freedom is innate. It is our spiritual breath. The body that breath animates is community. And here we are again with "I" and "We". "I" is just one letter in community, but without that letter, there is no community.

We must move forward together. When some fall, others help them up, knowing if not for the grace of God it could be themselves that had fallen.

We must move forward answering the call of Freedom which is vigilance. Defending our rights, defending the rights of others, and respecting the rights of those we may not agree with.

We must move forward embracing a future that lifts not just our generation, but the generations that follow. That most important American axiom: To give our children more than we had. To give our children that most incredible gift: To be an American. And to be free.

In the *Bhagavad-Gita* it lists the Divine Traits. Among them are these: truth, charity, honesty, loyalty, modesty, gentleness, patience, compassion, self-control, sacrifice, absence of anger, lack of greed. It says that these traits lead to freedom.

'The care of human life and happiness, and not their destruction, is the first and only object of good government.'
-Thomas Jefferson

No one gets left behind.

The Better Angels of Our Natures will not allow it. Because after all, when you save one life, you save the world.

CHAPTER EIGHT

Capital Radio

'Who ever controls the media, controls the mind.'
-Jim Morrison

'Media. I think I have heard of her. Isn't she the one who killed her children?'
-Neil Gaiman

Yellow Journalism and the Yellow Press are American terms for journalism and associated newspapers that present little or no legitimate, well-researched news while instead using eye-catching headlines for increased sales. Techniques may include exaggerations of news events, scandal mongering, or sensationalism. By extension, the term Yellow Journalism is used today as a pejorative to decry any journalism that treats news in an unprofessional or unethical fashion.[1]

Frank Luther Mott, 1939 Pulitzer-winning historian, identified Yellow Journalism with five characteristics: scare headlines in huge print, often of minor news; lavish use of pictures or imaginary drawings; use of faked interviews, misleading headlines, pseudoscience, a parade of false learning from so-called experts; emphasis on full-color Sunday supplements; dramatic sympathy with the "underdog" against the system. Frank would need a cardiologist if he had ever seen Social Media.

Everything described in the last two paragraphs is what the world is up against in trying to disseminate the information we colloquially call *"News"*. These dishonest practices have long been in use. The Spanish-American War is also known as the Newspaper War because of competing tabloids ratcheting-up the rhetoric to sell papers. Only now, in the Information Age, with the world quite literally in our back pant's pocket, this poison has a greater level of insidiousness and venom. And we, all of us, at some point, to some degree, take part in passing it along.

The anti-venom to Yellow Journalism and misinformation is knowledge. Sounds simple. It is.

Firstly, understand that you are being sold goods. *Info-tainment,* is the handle being thrown at what looks like "The News". Almost all news sources on all platforms are trying to grab your attention to sell their sponsor's products. Whether its television, radio, the Web, podcasts, magazines, newspapers, they are trying to draw your attention to sell you goods or services. "The News", mainstream and particularly alternative, has been reduced to that wacky inflatable, arms-waving tube man on used car lots. Everything that Mr. Mott described before World War 2 is very much in play today and on steroids. Its all *click-bait.*

Secondly, glean as much information as you can from as many sources as possible. Sources from *ALL* aspects of the political spectrum. Then, utilize your critical thinking skills to analyze the data and discern facts. Check your ego, hit pause on your emotions, approach the data sets like Spock, and formulate how these facts effect you, your family, your community, and the world at large.

This should seem extremely obvious, however, there seems to be a tremendous resurgence in non-critical thinking. In fact, the Medicine Show by the edge of town is drawing a rather large crowd and sales of Snake Oil are skyrocketing. The reasons for America's long fascination with the preposterous are many, and this isn't the place to delve into the socio-political, psychological causes and effects. The ramifications of so many people believing false narratives, misinformation, and outright lies are not just frightening, but deadly.

Thirdly, always check your sources. Find out who really owns the source of the information. As we saw in *The Dark Side* chapter, what on the surface seems like a legit source with legit information, may be wolves in shepherd's clothing. The answers to who owns what are one or two browser questions away from showing the man behind the curtain. For instance, The Weather Channel is owned by IBM. When you feel pinned to your couch because Winter Storm Yolanda is wreaking havoc across the upper Midwest, ask yourself if its really that awful. Because quite simply, its impossible to sell you soap if you're not planted in front of that television station or their app.

That's one rather benign *for-instance* that reflects how the information you are being handed is first manipulated in a board room, a place where quarterly bonuses are on everyone's minds.

What if in their greed the news-source doesn't care too much about getting a little loose with the facts. What if that boardroom has a *philosophy*; and the product they are selling *is* the philosophy.

We return to The Microphone, the Big Lie, and Nazi Germany. That awful history helps us to understand how powerful the Media is, and how frightening and deadly it can be. At-the-moment, in America, what might seem like a little white lie to generate a little extra income, what might seem like harmlessly hyping-up an issue to capture more viewers, what might look like an 'expert' from a source we trust, has become a significant problem that is eroding the very trust Americans have in the Media, the government, and in each other. Trust is the glue that holds society together. Short of massive physical violence and repression, the only way to divide this country is to use the Media to tear away the trust, the respect, *The Promise*.

Each of us holds the key to neutering the Media, and thereby thwarting those manipulating it. Data. Counterpoints to that data. Critical thinking. Check your sources. Follow the money. Look for the philosophy because that will tell you why they are trying to manipulate you.

One may ask, why isn't there a shepherd to knock the tar out of these wolves? There was. It was called the Fairness Doctrine and was introduced in 1949, furthering the Radio Act of 1927. The policy required the holders of broadcast licenses to both present controversial issues of public importance, and to do so in a manner that was honest, equitable, and balanced. Broadcasters had to air contrasting views regarding those controversial matters. The demise of this FCC rule has been considered by some to be a contributing factor for the rising level of party polarization.[2]

How did this demise happen? A back-and -forth between the FCC under Ronald Reagan-appointed Chairmen and Congress over whether the Fairness Doctrine violated the 1st Amendment, and whether the FCC was trying to flout Congress and therefore the People. In response to the FCC eliminating the Fairness Doctrine, Congress passed legislation attempting to codify/update the Doctrine. This was vetoed by President Reagan. President Bush threatened to veto it again four years later, thereby killing the bill and introducing a toxic can of worms into the ears and eyes of an unsuspecting nation.

It is no coincidence that one year later, ABC Radio signed Rush Limbaugh and ushered in an era of Talk Radio that contrary to fairness, decency, and honesty, began the division of our Country. Behavior that would have resulted in fines and licenses revoked, now has become the norm.

Jonathan Swift once said, 'Falsehood flies, and truth comes limping after it, so that when men come to be undeceived, it is too late; the jest is over, and the tale hath had its effect'. Imagine pounding those untruths over and over. Hour after hour. Year after year. Imagine sugar-coating those untruths with the most, base of comments, of appealing not to the Better Angels of our Natures, but rather to the most, vile. Dante understood this evil and placed Fraudulent Advisors in the Eighth Circle of Hell in his *Inferno*. So, should we.

Now imagine all of those elements just described: No rules, no fairness, no truth; profit before honesty, sensationalism before reality, lies compounded upon lies; and put all of that power to deceive into your phone.

Social Media has been described as addictive as alcohol and cigarettes. It has quite literally ruined people's lives. It is, as T.S. Eliot said, 'Distracted from distraction by distraction'.

It is also a formidable tool that has brought people and communities together, shared ideas and innovations, exposed crimes and criminals, shone light where once darkness prevailed, lifted spirits, sold one bezillion things, and given even the most marginalized a voice.

How does a society attempt to get their arms around so vast an entity? A free society? A society with a 1st amendment that guarantees free speech? We take the first tentative steps down a gray zone with these three quotes:

'For a nation that is afraid to let its people judge the truth and falsehood in an open market is a nation that is afraid of its people.'

-John F. Kennedy

'The American fascist would prefer not to use violence. His method is to poison the channels of public information.'
-Henry Wallace

'It's in our biology to trust what we see with our eyes. This makes living in a carefully edited, overproduced, and photoshopped world very dangerous.'
-Brené Brown

Yes, there should be some sort of shepherd to protect the flock. The Fairness Doctrine updated to this age and keeping artificial intelligence in mind. Rules that have been constructed by scientists with backgrounds in technology, communications, and public policy. Rules that are entirely devoid of politics. One only need look at Britain's Channel 4 Deepfake Christmas Message to realize how grave the situation with fake news is and can be. Misinformation happens now in real time, spread instantly by bots on multiple channels. The algorithms are designed to maximize connections. Connections equal people, and people equal sales. Morality isn't even a speed bump.

Ultimately, it falls on each one of us to apply critical thinking, check the sources, and understand that nearly all communication is a means to someone else's ends. We are our own administrators. No matter how sweet the message is that buttresses our beliefs, that message has been carefully crafted to sell us snake oil.

When the Nation's Capital was overrun by a mob on January 6th, 2021, all social media platforms kicked into hyperdrive to begin spinning, scrubbing, and flipping the objective data that was being carried out in front of our eyes. The agent provocateurs, bots, algorithms, talk radio hosts, newspapers, and television "news" shows were telling the American public that the overwhelming evidence in front of them was not what it looked like, but something else altogether. At the time of this writing, with a mountain of testimony from the perpetrators themselves, first-hand information from every level of law enforcement, and from the people inside the Capital Building, there are still human beings unconvinced of the bare facts. Human beings who are in Congress; human beings who report the news; human beings who may one day run for President of the United

States; human beings who are actively still perpetuating lies.[3]

The Art of The Lie and Yellow Journalism have been elevated to a level where the very fabric of our society is being called into question. How does a shepherd protect the flock when the sheep themselves have become wolves?

The solid, unbending, mathematical information that created the civilization we live in, teaches us to apply that same objectivity to the information we are bombarded with. This is critical thinking. If we want our freedoms, our civil liberties, our democracy to survive and be passed onto our children, then this skill is of paramount importance. Afterall, the price of freedom *is* eternal vigilance, even if we need be vigilant of our own selves.

At the same time, there needs to be laws preventing entities and individuals from screaming "fire" in a crowded theater. The common-sense line of free speech is crossed when its sole goal, besides profit, is stoking hatred and divisiveness to such a degree that common decency, honesty, and trust are trampled. The theologist and poet, Paul Gerhardt wrote, 'When a man lies, surely he murders some part of the world'. In these days of Yellow Journalism, Social Media, and alternate facts, those words resonate at a fevered pitch.

Our vigilance in this arena, as a people and as individuals, is paramount to the survival of America. Without each of us taking the time to look critically at the information in front of us, truth erodes. Where there is no truth, there is a vacuum waiting to be filled by malignant forces.

This is the forever war. This is the first line in the battle for freedom. And we are all soldiers or provocateurs, alternately, with each click.

'All truth passes through three stages. First, it is ridiculed. Second, it is violently opposed. Third, it is accepted as being self-evident.'
-Arthur Schopenhauer

'A lie can travel half-way around the world while the truth is putting on its shoes.'
-Mark Twain

'Though you cannot see when you fetch one step, what will be the next, yet follow truth, justice, and plain-dealing, and never

fear their leading you out of the labyrinth in the easiest manner possible.'
   -Thomas Jefferson

CHAPTER NINE

Grassroots

'That these dead shall not have died in vain. That this nation, under God, shall have a new birth of freedom and that government of the people, by the people, for the people, shall not perish from the earth.'
-Abraham Lincoln

'Just remember this, Mr. Potter, that this rabble you're talking about, they do most of the working and paying and living and dying in this community.'
-James Stewart *It's A Wonderful Life*

Government only works from the bottom up. No matter which political philosophy was employed from the Agricultural Revolution until the present day, every top-down system of government has ultimately failed. Those in absolute power tend to forget that their place at the top of the pyramid only exists because those at the base of the pyramid allow it.

There absolutely needs to be cohesion and organization in the political system. There certainly needs to be people empowered to make decisions throughout the entire system. And ultimately, there will always need to be someone who has the brave misfortune to be responsible for every decision and all the consequences. However, none of that happens without the collective will of the people.

Politically, it starts in the community at the grassroots level. The energy, the fresh ideas, the impetus, the will, drive, and force of politics is the buzz made by all the people working, living, paying bills, raising families, and creating thriving communities.

Participatory democracy is the hallmark of bottom-up. We the people vote for representatives to listen to our concerns and to vote for us at assemblies. It makes no difference if those assemblies are the local board of education, or the United States Senate. When those representing us fail to listen, we vote them out. If the representatives continue to ignore the collective will of the people, we switch political parties, create a new entity, or re-call/impeach. If this dissonance goes on then we have the right to assemble, strike, march, boycott, and any number of other tactics in-order-to get our voices heard.

The virus that smokes this complex organism is complacency. When we make that *Promise* to be Americans, though we have the right to be as lazy as we want to be, all we're really doing is leaving a festering mess for someone else to clean up. Our participation keeps the organism alive and healthy. Our complacency only serves to allow parasites a way in.

The Constitution sets up the framework for this organism to function and to correct itself. It does this while attempting to keep mob rule at bay, and to also discourage minority rule. The Constitution was a direct bottom-up solution from citizens exploited by various British top-down models, be that model Companies, Proprietors, or direct Monarchy. All three of those British attempts to govern the Colonies were top-down, and all three failed.[1] The Constitution, and thereby the

Country, counts on the citizens of the Country to participate in its governance. The citizens elect the representatives to create the laws that guide the nation, protect the people, and their property. Hence, the nation of laws that America is.

The gum in the machine to this not-so-perfect but seems-to-work system are the political parties and their national committees. The essentially two-party system in American politics survives by laws, party rules, and customs that were never laid out in the Constitution.

In theory, these two monolithic entities, the political parties along with their national committees, are responsible to their members for the selection of candidates, creation of policy, and the political direction/philosophy of either the Democratic or Republican Party.

In reality, these two monolithic entities are corrupted top-down by special interest's slush-funding, and then forced to the extreme edges of philosophy by mob-rule from the bottom-up.

In this time of extreme divisiveness, it has become increasingly difficult to find Common Sense, compromise, and fact-based rational argument; it has become increasingly difficult for the two parties to put *Country* before party. That power-hungry, greed-inspired feeling emanating from the two parties is indicative of top-down, and it will take a herculean, face-to-face approach from the Democratic National Committee and the Republican National Committee to regain the trust of The People. Given the myriad challenges facing any nation in the best of times, every year that is wasted by these two monolithic entities in not connecting with the citizens only serves to weaken America. Thus, the growing number of voters aligning themselves as independent[2], and the sinking approval ratings of congress. Although much of this angst felt toward the two parties has been well-earned, the endless negative diatribe from the extreme right about government has hyper-fueled an already volatile situation, coupled with a media that thrives on negative news.

'We hold these truths to be self-evident, that all men are created equal.'

This is the single greatest sentence ever written in the course of human history. When we think of 'grassroots' we think about common cause uniting citizens to stand up against egregious acts. We think of marches in the streets, fists in the air, signs lifted above heads. We think about door-to-door efforts to get folks registered to vote, of petitions being signed, of packed city council halls. These and more are our rights guaranteed to us in the Constitution. These rights are why we must be vigilant, and they are also *how* we can be vigilant.

In the history of the United States, there is no single movement that is greater, nor defines the essence of 'grassroots' better, than the Civil Rights Movement. As the American Revolution inspired the world to throw off the yoke of tyranny, the American Civil Rights Movement inspired peoples around the world to make good on those norm-shattering words: *All men are created equal.*

The very essence of America is embodied in the egalitarian, grassroots approach that fueled both the American Revolution and the Civil Rights Movement. The fight to ensure those unalienable rights and the fight to ensure equal rights is ongoing. Without our constant vigilance, as individuals being aware and engaging in the democratic process, or by watchdog organizations both inside the government and independent of the government, the wolves of tyranny and oppression slip in.

Americans are not bound together by race, religion, or a single culture. Americans cannot be defined in single descriptive words. The esprit d' corps that brings us all together are the two concepts of *unalienable rights* and that *all men are created equal.* Combined those equal freedom. Combined those equal liberty. What may seem rabble to kings, is a diaspora with an unconquerable will to be free.

'Give me your tired, your poor, your huddled masses yearning to be free.' America is a nation of underdogs. Of fighters. Of human beings that have seen enough of despots and are willing to risk everything for just a chance. We are the grassroots.

Without this river of energy coming to these shores America would not be what it is. Without the living memory of how bad things can be in autocratic governments, America would not be evolving. Without evolution there is only death. The collective energy and will of the American people, from those stepping off the boat to those whose ancestors walked across the land bridge, is what fires Lady Liberty's torch. *We are America.*

It is up to us to ensure that this nation remains a democratic republic. That the laws created in this nation protect all of us, work for all of us, and ultimately, unite all of us. This happens from the grassroots up. This happens by citizens engaging in their communities. Alexander the Great said it best, 'Upon the conduct of each depends the fate of all'.

Economically, it also starts in the community at the grassroots level.

The key to America's success in the past was a continent of natural resources coupled with an enduring drive to prosper on the part of millions of refugees. The key to America's success in the future will be that enduring drive to prosper by millions of Americans coupled with the unlimited resources of our minds. This quantum leap of ideas, energy, engagement, prosperity, and problem-solving only takes place with a bottom-up approach.

The intentions behind laissez faire economics are earnest: allow free enterprise to create, grow, expand, push, and prosper. The intentions behind Keynesian economics are likewise earnest: have enough centralized control over the economy to avoid wild fluctuations, monopolization, and other massive disruptions that would create chaos, hardship, and poverty. Somewhere in the middle of these two warring factions, in that wonderful zone known as Common Sense, lies the solution.

There is a third type of economics called Distributism that believes economic success begins at the grassroots/community level.

According to Distributists, the right to property is a fundamental right and the means of production should be spread as widely as possible rather than being centralized under the control of the state (state capitalism), a few individuals (plutocracy), or corporations (corporatocracy). Therefore, distributism advocates a society marked by widespread property ownership. Cooperative economist Race Mathews argues that such a system is key to bringing about a just social order.[3]

Distributism points out that in socialism the state owns all the means of production and the property; and that in laissez faire capitalism a handful of wealthy individuals/corporations own most of the means of production/property and use that wealth to buy/influence the state. Distributism further points out that all other models of economics are founded on the belief that economics is a science and can therefore be measured and applied. Whereas Distributism believes that economics is a type of relationship between humans and therefore is unpredictable. It states that economics has more to do with ethics than money, and that the only way for economics to be fair throughout a society is to spread the property and the means of production as widely as possible throughout that society.

Local cooperatives, family businesses, and laws that favor these over large corporations are hallmarks of Distributism. There is an emphasis on free trade, worker's rights, and the ability for families and communities to take care of themselves. The two fundamental principles that drive this theory are subsidiarity and solidarity. The Oxford English Dictionary defines subsidiarity as 'the principle that a central authority should have a subsidiary function, performing only those tasks which cannot be performed at a more local level'. The same dictionary defines solidarity as 'unity or agreement of feeling or action, especially among individuals with a common interest; mutual support within a group'.

The difference between laissez faire capitalism, Keynesian capitalism, and socialism with Distributism is that the ownership of property and the means of production is widely distributed amongst the citizens, *and* there are laws protecting those citizens, their businesses, and their property. Grassroots. The American Dream.

Here again the principle of subsidiarity must be respected: a community of a higher order should not interfere in the internal life of a community of a lower order, depriving the latter of its functions, but rather should support it in case of need and help to coordinate its activity with the activities of the rest of society, always with a view to the common good.[4]

-Pope John Paul II

No civilization survives without its middle class. In order to nurture, sustain, and grow the middle class, the grassroots fundamental principles of unalienable rights, equal rights, and widely distributed wealth have to be promoted and protected. The single most important unit of community in anyone's life is their family. Economics, and the politics and laws that govern economics, must emphasize the family first, then the union/local association, then the city/town/village, then the county, then the region, the state, and finally the federal government. Societies grow from the bottom up. Societies always fail from the top down. Whether the wealth is centralized in the state, or with 650-plus billionaires, (the top 1% of America owns more wealth than the entire middle class[5]), it is only a matter of time before the eventual disparity in wealth crushes the middle class and violence ensues. History has taught us this endlessly.

Main Street, the 'real economy', is vastly more important than Wall Street to most Americans. Trickle down economics and massive tax breaks for the wealthy only results in economic disparity, federal debt, hardship, and resentment. The reinvestment of wealth into capital at the local level is pivotal. Taxes should be skewed to promote local lending institutions. Laws should be tilted in favor of small business. Zoning should be created to promote local businesses and not mega-chains.

The foundation of society is cemented by human interaction. Anyone who has ever owned a business understands that business is about relationships first. Even if you have fire-in-a-bottle, the failure to cultivate successful relationships will doom that business eventually. So, it is with all human endeavors. Economics is a series of transactions that mark a relationship. Of all the types of capital that exist, human capital is the most important.

Grassroots. America started with a ragtag collection of disenfranchised human beings who in their desperation answered to a higher call. Though they collectively did not live by the words they fought for, as evidenced by slavery, the continual war against the Native Americans, and the relegation of women to second-class citizens, the movement they started has changed the course of the human race.

Grassroots. The spark of the Constitution, *all men are created equal*, lit a fire that has swept the planet. When Martin Luther King stood on the steps of the Lincoln Memorial and told the world of his dream, he spoke for every blade of grass, for every human from antiquity to ages in the future.

Grassroots. The American Dream lives inside each of us as the enduring spirit to not simply survive, but to thrive. The businesses we create, the careers we develop, the achievements, accolades, and material possessions we accumulate, they are the props upon the stage of the powerful play as we recite our verse.

Family. Community. Our hometown. Our neck of the woods. The State we live in. America. The world grows from the ground up.

Our roots are wonderfully tangled together. In no small way, we hold each other up. In no small way, it is upon our backs that civilization exists at all.

'Alone we can do so little; together we can do so much.'
-Helen Keller

'Heaven sees as the people see; heaven hears as the people hear.'
-Mencius

CHAPTER TEN

Free and Fair

One human, one vote. The most votes wins. Those votes determine the direction of the country. It sure sounds simple. Fairly certain this was the intention when all that expensive tea found its way into Boston Harbor. Representation which in fact, represents the citizenry. However, in America's nearly quarter millennium of existence, who gets to vote and what stands in their way of voting has been a long and twisted tale of voter repression.

Everyone has the right to take part in the government of his country, directly or through freely chosen representatives. The will of the people shall be the basis of the authority of government; this will shall be expressed in periodic and genuine elections which shall be by universal and equal suffrage and shall be held by secret vote or by equivalent free voting procedures.

-Article 21, Universal Declaration of Human Rights, 1948

Voting is the cornerstone of democracy. The more free-and-fair the elections are, the stronger the democracy. What plagues this simple calculation are the manipulations of calculating men. The concept of *Universal Suffrage* means that every adult citizen has the right to vote regardless of race, gender, ethnicity, religion, physical disability, sexual orientation, property considerations, or level of education. It means that nothing should stand in the way of voting: no fee, no poll tax, no physical barriers, no great or unreasonable distance to travel, no intimidation and or threat of violence. Again, this seems remarkably obvious, but again, in the history of America, right up to the very moment these words are being written, voter repression continues to take place.

In, *The Dark Side,* we touched on Citizens United v. the Federal Election Commission and how the unlimited amounts of untraceable Dark Money have upended and sullied the integrity of American elections. We spoke on how *Project Redmap* and gerrymandering have done the same. Twice the House of Representatives has passed a bill, H.R. 1 (116th Congress) and H.R. 1 (117th Congress), that would clean-up the election process and return the very principles of free and fair elections. In 2019 the bill never saw the Senate floor to even be debated on. In 2021 at the time of this writing, it will likely be killed before debate as the 60 votes needed to bypass the filibuster do not exist.

In a new national poll released today by Data for Progress and Equal Citizens, 67% of Americans say they support H.R.1 For the People Act, even after being provided opposition messaging. This support continued across party lines: a majority of Republican (56%), Independent (68%), and Democratic voters (77%) also support H.R.1. 67% of national likely voters support H.R.1 | 13% don't know | 19% oppose.[1]

Why then, with such overwhelming support for this bill from the people the senators represent, would they not enact this bill into law? For the same reasons that America has struggled against itself since the ink was wet on the Constitution: the vested interests of a small handful of greedy men.

Its difficult to be the shining city on the hill, when the lights of democracy are sporadically covered in the blood of its own citizens. The People forged this Union of States. Their collective will should determine that Union's course. The blatant disregard of the collective will of the American People by duly elected officials is why distrust in the American Government is at an all time high.[2] Citizens on all sides of the political divide understand that money, influence, tilted laws, and outright greed, are stealing democracy from the American people. Hence, the broad-based support for H.R. 1.

This is the most important issue facing America. Without campaign finance reform, without an end to gerrymandering, without free and fair elections embracing universal suffrage, the slide into an oligarchy and eventual dictatorship is inevitable. It is so important to remember the connection between the American industrial elite and Nazi Germany. It is equally important to understand the repressive racial history of the United States, the lives lost defending the basic rights of American workers, and the never-ending wars America fights in the interests of those same few, greedy men.

As a nation, Americans are good people. The solid, helping, loving, caring, forgiving, striving, working, living, deeply patriotic citizens of this country deserve better representation than what they are currently receiving. They certainly deserve better sources of information. At the very least they deserve to be told the truth. The American people are asking the two political parties to put aside their money-influenced special interests and make decisions based on what the people want.

In this day-and-age, voting should be remarkably easy and secure. The layers of security that protect Bitcoin shows a blueprint on protecting elections. The Covid-19 pandemic showed how simple it is to remote nearly every aspect of life. The endless lines at remote precincts to vote is an anachronism. The folks holding onto this anachronism, and even making it more difficult to vote, are doing so to protect the Corporate Elite they work for.[3]

The simple truth is that elections in America are more secure than ever.[4] *'The Big Lie'* that was perpetuated by President Trump in the 2020 American Presidential Election, that there was widespread fraud resulting in his loss, has been debunked at every level, thrown out of every courtroom, and only served to further cleave an already, and conveniently, divided nation. From the ashes of that election will arise a phoenix of democracy. What four years of unmitigated lies, graft, and division destroyed, combined with the public response to extrajudicial killings of unarmed citizens, and the stresses of the Covid-19 pandemic, has created an America that has a renewed respect and awareness for truth, justice, and that all human beings are created equal. The fear of this engaged citizenry is what is compelling the Corporate Elite to suppress voting. Likewise, at the behest of that Corporate Elite, the subterfuge in the Senate regarding H.R. 1 and its defeat.

Let the people vote. It is the cornerstone of our Democratic Republic. Make it as simple and easy as possible. Make election day a national holiday. End gerrymandering by applying a uniform system for all states so that districts can only encompass whole counties or parishes, rather than looking like children used a Spirograph. If a picture ID is needed, then the onus to produce this is with the government, door-to-door, citizen by citizen if necessary. Campaign finance reform returns the power to the people. Every donation should be public. All Dark Money eliminated and made illegal. In-order-to wrangle in the obscene costs of campaigns, the election cycle should be shortened.

There is no reason any longer for behind-closed-doors politicking, whether this is for elections or to influence policy. We live in an age of digitized media, automation, social media, and incredibly powerful cell phones. Every meeting between lobbyists and politicians should be in a public space, recorded, and instantly made available for anyone to view.

Bills have been proposed and bills have been defeated, at all levels of government, to implement these common-sense solutions to a corruption problem in America that goes back to the 18th century. Two things stand in the way of truth and common sense: the lawmakers themselves and the folks interpreting the laws.

'Freedom and justice cannot be parceled out in pieces to suit political convenience. I don't believe you can stand for freedom for one group of people and deny it to others.'
-Coretta Scott King

'Judges are the weakest link in our system of justice, and they are also the most protected.'
-Alan Dershowitz

A judge is a person who presides over court proceedings, either alone or as a part of a panel of judges. The powers, functions, method of appointment, discipline, and training of judges vary widely across different jurisdictions. The judge is supposed to conduct the trial impartially and, typically, in an open court.[5]

No matter what laws are passed, at the end of the day, if someone or some entity doesn't like the laws as they stand, with enough money they can challenge those laws right up to the Supreme Court. There, at the highest court in the land, there is no jury. There are nine justices who decide the cases they choose to place in front of them. Those nine justices sit on this court for life. These nine human beings are the weakest link in our system. Own them and you own the whole shooting match.

There has of late been a movement amongst the judiciary, a philosophical change from impartiality to activism. A philosophy that takes the blindfold off justice and replaces it with blinders, or rather, with a political prism to run laws through. When this activism is coupled with a political/judicial philosophy called 'originalism' pertaining to interpreting the Constitution in its purest, 'original' form, then you no longer have a court, you have a tribunal.

Here are several quotes from Thomas Jefferson regarding the Constitution, the judiciary, and the Supreme Court:

'Some men look at Constitutions with sanctimonious reverence and deem them like the ark of the covenant, too sacred to be touched. They ascribe to the men of the preceding age a wisdom more than human and suppose what they did to be beyond amendment. I

knew that age well; I belonged to it and labored with it. It deserved well of its country. It was very like the present but without the experience of the present; and forty years of experience in government is worth a century of book-reading; and this they would say themselves were they to rise from the dead.'

'I am not an advocate for frequent changes in laws and Constitutions. But laws and institutions must go hand in hand with the progress of the human mind. As that becomes more developed, more enlightened, as new discoveries are made, new truths discovered and manners and opinions change, with the change of circumstances, institutions must advance also to keep pace with the times. We might as well require a man to wear still the coat which fitted him when a boy as civilized society to remain ever under the regimen of their barbarous ancestors.'

'I consider trial by jury as the only anchor ever yet imagined by man, by which a government can be held to the principles of its constitution.'

'If some period be not fixed, either by the Constitution or by practice, to the services of the First Magistrate, his office, though nominally elective, will, in fact, be for life, and that will soon degenerate into an inheritance.'

'The moral sense is as much a part of our Constitution as that of feeling, seeing, or hearing.'

'The judiciary of the United States is the subtle corps of sappers and miners constantly working under ground to undermine the foundations of our confederated fabric. They are construing our Constitution from a co-ordination of a general and special government to a general and supreme one alone.'

'The Constitution... meant that its coordinate branches should be checks on each other. But the opinion which gives to the judges the right to decide what laws are constitutional and what not, not only for themselves in their own sphere of action but for the Legislature and Executive also in their spheres, would make the Judiciary a despotic branch.'

In the words of one of our principal Founding Fathers, he, and they, never wanted it to be set in stone, held up on an altar, or to be so entrenched as to not reflect the times. They tried to create a Constitution that would be difficult to amend, but at the same time could be flexible as times and people changed. The spirit of the document, its primary intent, shines through in its opening words:

We the People of the United States, in Order to form a more perfect Union, establish Justice, insure domestic Tranquility, provide for the common Defence, promote the general Welfare, and secure the Blessings of Liberty to ourselves and our Posterity, do ordain and establish this CONSTITUTION for the United States of America.

Let us be frank: the rest of the document is an owner's manual. If the government or powerful sections of American society are not establishing Justice, insuring domestic Tranquility, providing for common Defence, promoting the general Welfare, and securing the Blessings of Liberty for this generation and those to follow, then perhaps an upgrade is necessary, and an improved owner's manual to accompany the changes. That was the intention of our Founding Fathers.

The 'originalist' movement/philosophy and its rigid interpretation of the Constitution is not only in the judiciary but is also pervasive throughout American society. These folks, as duty sworn as they may be, as enamored with the Constitution as it was written in 1787, have handcuffed society to exactly what our Founding Fathers did *not* want to happen. Even the lightest reading in Natural History will tell you that an inability to evolve results in stagnation and death.

Controversy has stalked the hallowed halls of the Supreme Court since nearly its inception. From Marbury v Madison (1803) where the Court asserted its power, through Dred Scott v Sandford (1857) where the Court determined that African-Americans have no Constitutional Rights, through Plessy v Ferguson (1896) when the Court determined that African-Americans were separate but equal, up to Bush v Gore (2000) where the outcome of a Presidential election was determined on a 5 to 4 vote, and including the Citizens United v the Federal Election Commission (2010) in which the Court decided that corporations have the same rights as citizens, the Supreme Court has a long history of jaw-dropping decisions. It would be overly simplistic to characterize the Court as a rubber stamp for American business interests, however, much of that statement would stick.

Because the Justices themselves, as well as judges at all levels, affiliate themselves with a political party, they thereby nullify their impartiality. Because America is a nation of laws, thereby making laws so vital and the role of judges so important, the judiciary system could use some fine tuning. Without devolving into a lengthy and esoteric tome on how to fix the American judicial system, here is one suggestion for the Supreme Court that might just fix the mess lock, stock, and barrel: term limits.

Every President, during-the-course of their four-year term, gets to appoint two justices. The oldest two justices currently serving are retired to make room for the two newly appointed justices. Thus, the people have elected the President, and the President appoints two justices. This is the simplest way to return the Supreme Court to the people for whom they serve.

Much has been said of expanding the number of justices on the Supreme Court. This would help to better reflect American society. There is a strong argument for this in all aspects and levels of government. When one realizes that the 117th Congress is over 80% male, 70% white, and one-third are over 65 years of age[6], then one can ascertain that in a society where these demographics are quite different, perceptions of reality between these two groups is going to be radically at odds.

There also needs to be more stringent requirements in who gets to serve on the Supreme Court. The incredible power and importance of a seat on the Supreme Court should not be taken lightly. The persons who occupy these seats should have years of experience. They should be as purely impartial as possible, without any obvious associations to political institutions.

The last Justice appointed at the time of this writing, Justice Amy Coney Barret, sat as a judge for a grand total of three years. By comparison, apprenticeship in the building trades may take between two and five years, it takes up to seven years of residency to become a doctor, and it can take ten years before one earns their black belt in kung fu. It should also be noted that Ms. Barret was a member of, and endorsed by, the Federalist Society, a Koch-financed, originalist/neo-liberalist organization.[7] The advertising campaign for her nomination, a tip-off to chicanery right there, was endorsed to the tune of over $1,000,000 by The Americans For Prosperity Foundation[8], likewise a Koch-funded Dark Money entity.

Benjamin Franklin once wrote: 'I grew convinced that truth, sincerity, and integrity in dealings between man and man were of the utmost importance to the felicity of life.' Therein is what we the people expect from the judges that work for us; an honest interpretation of the law, a sincerity that speaks of impartiality, and an integrity where all sides of a case can expect a fair trial.

These are the three things that dovetail together to make Free and Fair: A Constitution that stands on its principles and still can change with the times as Thomas Jefferson envisioned it; universal and equal suffrage free from Dark Money; and an impartial, unbiased judiciary. Quite simply, without all three of these it is only a matter of time before our Democratic Republic is replaced with something autocratic.

Understanding what is going on is not 'politics.' 'Politics,' has been made an ugly word in-an-effort to get fewer people involved with the infrastructures and mechanisms that impact our lives. The people/institutions doing this have a vested interest in your not being involved: money and power. Understanding the Constitution-your rights, understanding what is universal and equal suffrage-your fundamental right for sincere representation, and understanding Congress/Judiciary/Supreme Court-how laws are being made and how they are being interpreted, are the most valuable tools you have as an American. With this understanding you can act. Whether the actions you take are to serve, volunteer, protest, educate, or simply to vote, understanding is the key. Being aware is the key. Knowledge is power, and that is precisely why those greedy few do not want you to have that knowledge.

'Honesty is the first chapter in the book of wisdom,' said Thomas Jefferson. *Free and Fair* is what the American Constitution emulated for this Democratic Republic. It is plain to see in current American events which people/institutions are living up to this ideal. It is up to us *The People,* the vested authority in this Democratic Republic, to hold those entities/institutions that aren't living up to the ideal of free and fair, accountable. We can do so by understanding, serving, volunteering, protesting, educating, boycotting, and voting. If the lion's share of Americans simply took one business week off together, and stopped purchasing non-essentials, the screams from the Corporate Elite would be deafening.

'One man with courage is a majority', said Thomas Jefferson. Imagine 330,000,000 Americans with courage.

CHAPTER ELEVEN

Flashpoints

'A good compromise is one where everybody makes a contribution.'
-Angela Merkel

There are issues that are so divisive, so emotive, so deeply and passionately held, that the mere mention of those issues elicits responses that fail common sense. These are flashpoints. They are the stumbling blocks, the roadblocks, the traps, that impede progress. They are also the issues that are painfully easy to exploit in-order-to divide the nation.

Throwing caution to the wind, we will pull the gauze aside and examine these open-wound, push-button, knee-jerk, issues to find some common-sense middle ground where compromise exists. Because, if we simply agree to disagree, nothing will ever get done. If nothing gets done, it leaves an opening for all sorts of parasites to enter.

Abortion.

The essence of this issue has been completely trampled in political rhetoric. It has been used to divide a nation. The incredibly difficult, complex decision of a mother to abort their unborn child has been hijacked by the political interests of the Democrats and the Republicans and the people that own those two parties.

The essence of this issue is deeply personal. Though America has laws to protect the vulnerable, it does not have a history of doing so. Though America is a nation of laws, is it possible to legislate morality? (Prohibition and the war on drugs mark two epic failures.) Is it possible in a sweeping nation-wide law, or in fifty-different states-wide laws, to legislate abortion, and solve an issue that has existed for thousands of years?

No matter when you think life begins for a human being, what is the best, most common-sense way to find a compromise on this issue. The essence of both arguments on this issue are based in compassion. That is where the common ground lies. That is where a solution in a legislative sense exists.

Abortion should still be legal. It should not be allowed after a certain time in the pregnancy because it is no longer safe, unless the mother's life is in danger. Those entities that want to make abortion illegal should refocus their energies into connecting with and supporting the mothers who are considering abortion.

The solution to ending abortions and preserving life is in reaching out to the hearts of expecting mothers. The support, physically, emotionally, and economically, of those mothers until the birth of the child results in in their keeping the baby or in adoption. In addition, the positive outcome of those two lives past the point of birth is also a part of the process.

Pro-life is just that: pro-life. All life. At every stage of life. Those are dramatically difficult words to live by without being hypocritical. Perhaps being pro-life is an entirely different argument than whether abortion is legal or illegal. Perhaps the most common-sense way to address so thorny an issue is to realize that the roses amongst those thorns are the mother and the child. How best do we compassionately aid them both?

Non-governmental organizations such as churches, working with Planned Parenthood, clinics, and doctors that perform abortions, with funding from the government coupled with donations from the NGO's, connect with expecting mothers. Adoption agencies, foster homes, and social workers are also linked into the process.

What has been achieved with this connection respects the decision of the mother and the life of the child. By reaching out to the mother before an abortion can legally take place, all the options, consequences, and costs, (spiritual, physical, emotional, economic), have been addressed. Ultimately, in a nation that so ardently believes in personal freedom, it is the mother's decision. Her heart is where the connection needs to be made, not in the media, not in the backrooms of the DNC or the RNC, and not by legislative bodies comprised overwhelmingly of men.

Gun Control.

A well-regulated militia, being necessary to the security of a free state, the right of the people to keep and bear arms, shall not be infringed.

This fiercely, frequently, and erroneously misinterpreted line from the 2nd Amendment, is what let the genie out of the bottle. The logic of this sentence, what the framers of the Constitution meant, is not ambiguous. It is not a mystery. It is not an open-ended agreement for citizens to own all manner of lethality. The logic of this sentence can be simply shown by breaking it down in a sentence tree.

The subject of this sentence is: *A well-regulated militia.* The verb phrase of this sentence is: *the right of the people to keep and bear arms, shall not be infringed.* In other words, the sole reason for the citizenry to keep and bear arms is in case the country is invaded and all citizens, who at the time of the writing of the Constitution were citizen-soldiers, were needed in the country's defense.

The well-regulated militia does not give every citizen the right to form a militia. The well-regulated militia is sanctioned and controlled by the government that the citizens have elected.

Any other interpretation of this sentence in the 2nd Amendment invites chaos. And so, here we are.

Two out of three Americans supports stricter gun laws. Three-quarters of Americans support a 3-day wait before the firearm can be taken home. Seventy percent support the idea of a national data base for gun sales.[1]

In 1787, when the Constitution was written, a flintlock musket had the magazine capacity of one round with an effective range of 50 meters. The round would leave the musket with a muzzle velocity of 1000 feet per second. An experienced rifleman could get off three rounds in one minute.

In 2021, an AR-15 has a magazine capacity of thirty rounds with an effective range of 550 meters, and a muzzle velocity of 3,260 feet per second. An inexperienced human can still get off over forty-five rounds per minute.

In 1787, the thirteen states comprising the United States of America were essentially on the frontier. Citizens who did not live in a major town were in the hinterland. They needed that musket to put food on the table.

In 2021, unless one has chosen to find what is left of the hinterland to homestead on, food is remarkably easy to find.

At a rate of 4.43 deaths per 100,000 people, gun violence in the United States is four times higher than the rates in war-torn Syria and Yemen.[2]

No other nation suffers as much gun violence as does the United States. Common Sense dictates that something needs to be done. The citizens of the nation overwhelmingly support stricter gun laws. At what point do we put the health and well being of the community, over a personal freedom produced by misinterpreting the 2nd Amendment.

Thomas Jefferson stated how our Constitution must reflect the changes that have happened as mankind and the nation modernizes. Most Americans understand what he meant by this and how it relates to the 2nd Amendment. They understand that stricter gun laws do not take people's guns away.

A minority of people, less than one-third of the adult population, owns a firearm. Twenty percent of the adult American population owns more than one firearm.[3] Three percent of Americans own more than half the country's guns.[4] This is hardly a political juggernaut that politicians should be cowering in fear from.

So, what exactly is the wall that all this logic runs into? An originalist-interpretation of the Constitution that thinly veils greed, a political slush fund of graft and corruption on the part of the firearms lobby that buys favors contrary to the will of the American people, and a lack of moral courage on the part of politicians on the take.

Because of gerrymandering, the filibuster, and Dark Money, stricter gun laws in America face an uphill battle. The simple solution to this issue is to recognize the obvious logic and protect the country from itself. Remember, Thomas Jefferson said: *The care of human life and happiness, and not their destruction, is the first and only object of good government.*

If it continues to prove so daunting to pass common sense legislation that both protects citizens, and their right to own firearms, then gun violence should be seen as a health crisis. As gun violence is staggeringly expensive, perhaps tearing away the protective laws harboring firearm manufacturers should be stripped, thereby allowing class-action lawsuits. This methodology has proven effective regarding the tobacco industry, energy and chemical production industries, the pharmaceutical industry, and agriculture and food industries. If the politicians the nation elects cannot protect the care and happiness of the citizenry, then unbiased courts may provide an arena of fair justice.

Taxes.

After voting, the most essential service we render when we make *The Promise to be an American,* is to pay our taxes. The price tag for the freedoms, the infrastructure, and the security we have is the monies charged us by the government. Taxes equal civilization. There is no other way around it. The return on investment is astonishingly good, considering how many blessings we have as Americans, no matter how distasteful it may be to write those tax checks.

There is also no other way to make the entirety of 'nationhood' possible. The Neoliberalist mantra is to eliminate government and privatize all services. All this would do is result in despotic corporate-rulers, lousy infrastructure, taxation through pricing, and eventually huge, monolithic monopolies. In a word: autocracy.

Pay your taxes. Pay them with pride. Each-and-every day, every one of us takes full advantage of an America that would stagger the minds of the Founding Fathers.

The problem with taxation lies in fairness. Many have argued for a flat rate tax system. It simply won't work. One-third of a $30,000 annual income reduces that person to poverty. One-third of an annual income of 1,000,000 is less than what would be owed currently.

The progressive graduated system in place is as fair a system as there is. The issues with it are four-fold: 1) The tax rate at the highest levels of earnings isn't steep enough, 2) The corporate tax rate isn't steep enough, 3) The loopholes that exist where the wealthy/corporations pay next to nothing, 4) The inability of the Internal Revenue Service to enforce fraud and collect what is owed the country.

In 1956 the federal income tax rate for individuals making more than $300,000, ($2,900,000 in 2021 monies[5]), was 91%. That is unfair on the high side. In 2020, the federal income tax rate for individuals making $2,900,000 is 37%. That is unfair on the low side.

When you own a business there are two ways to shepherd your money: Cash flow into the business and cash flow out of the business. There is only so much you can do to control cash flow out of the business. You can only reduce labor and tighten systems so much before you degrade your services/product. Cash flow into the business, in theory, is limitless.

Business sense, logic, and fairness determine that the following corrections to the tax system must be implemented. Federal levels of taxation for the very wealthy need to be raised to 45%. State income taxes should be the same across the country, leveling the playing field and creating an atmosphere of cooperation instead of competition. The corporate tax rate needs to be raised to above 30%. All monies earned by corporations must be taxed. If they are trying to move that money overseas, then it gets taxed at the corporate tax rate before it leaves the country. A universal, global corporate tax rate needs to be set so that Tax Shelters no longer exist and the temptation to cheat the United States of

America is no longer an option. Red, White, and Blue for one, is Red, White, and Blue for all. Pay your taxes.

All loopholes, deductions, and corporate subsidies need to be closed or eliminated. The standard deduction is it. Streamlining the tax process streamlines the I.R.S. freeing them up to go get the cheaters. Will it eliminate the jobs of some accountants? Much fewer than the internet already has. Those individuals whose situations have been made redundant can apply to the Criminal Investigation Division of the I.R.S. and go get those cheaters.

It is impossible to run a business without income. You can't keep the lights to the Shining City lit without the monies to supply the juice. Along with voting, taxation is a cornerstone of democracy.

The National Debt exists partially from over-spending, (cash flow out), but mostly from lack of revenue, (cash flow in). Supply side economics by and of itself does not work. Like communism, it fails to account for human nature. The monies do not trickle down, and they do not end up in government coffers. Logic dictates that you cannot lower both the highest personal tax brackets and the corporate tax, and still expect to fund the nation. Incentive to invest is created by forcing private enterprise to re-invest its money inside the corporation, not in Wall Street, not in outsized salaries and bonuses, and certainly not overseas. If monies are not reinvested through strict regulation back into their business' infrastructure, then it is taxed.

Only fools and thieves choke off the revenue stream to a business, and then criticize the business for being inept.

The National Debt

There is no way to discuss the United States National Debt without first talking about taxes, and how the cash flow into the Federal coffers was slashed during the Reagan administration. One of the principal tenets of Movement Conservatism/Neo-liberalism is to lower the tax rate on the wealthy and corporations. The gamble is that the wealthy and corporations will reinvest these monies back into their businesses, into the community, and inside the country.

They didn't. In fact, there is a sharp correlation between tax cuts and the National

Debt.[6] While income tax has remained about half of all Federal revenue, corporate and excise taxes, (the federal excise tax on gasoline hasn't been raised since 1993[7]) have plummeted as a percentage of that revenue[8]. Had they kept pace with income taxes as a percentage of revenue, in other words not been slashed, an estimated amount of over 4 trillion dollars in revenue would have been raised. This figure represents one-seventh of the current National Debt as of April 2021, (28 trillion dollars).

Obviously, the above figure is staggering and is a real-world problem. Obviously, one-seventh is only a seventh, but for anyone who has had to manage a debt-load, that's real money. Equally obvious, is that America needs to get its fiscal house in order.

Cash flow in, is the first place to start. Then, raise the corporate tax rate, close the loopholes, and no longer allow corporate inversions.[9] Spending $700 billion a year on defense is next. The United States spends more on defense than the next ten countries combined.[10] Eliminating all corporate subsidies is third. Not including tax loopholes, this amounts to about $100 billion a year, an almost impossible number to nail because there is little transparency regarding corporate welfare. Certainly, investing in research and development is pivotal, but giving money to for-profit industries flies in the face of a by-the-bootstraps philosophy.

Strategically, practically, and fiscally, the United States of America has a debt issue that could sink the nation. Clear, concise information unsullied by politics must be utilized to adopt a clear and formative response to this problem. There can be no more deficits, and the debt must begin to be paid down. This will take several generations. The only legislative solution to this is a Constitutional Amendment. That is how huge the problem is, and how daunting solving it will be. After World War Two, the National Debt was 113% of GDP. By the late 1970's, it was reduced to 25% of GDP. In that timeframe, are the answers to addressing this issue. As with all these flashpoints, it takes courage and the will to face them.

Defense Spending

$731.75 billion is a lot of money. That was the amount allocated to defense/military spending in 2019[11]. This annual expenditure, and the truncated cash flow coming in as federal revenue, are the reasons why we can't have nice things.

Benjamin Franklin once said that 'an ounce of prevention is worth a pound of cure'. Nowhere is this more, true than in the arena of defense. A solid strategic national plan that spans administrations, diplomacy, treaties, and solid intelligence solve nearly all problems before a shot need be fired. A clear understanding that 'defense' is not 'offence', and that the strategic interests of the United States is not protecting fossil fuels for American corporations.

Having said that, negotiating from a position of strength makes things a whole lot easier. The military might of the United States is unparalleled in human history. Maintaining that is expensive. Chasing ideas and technologies is expensive. The key is to have a long-term plan. The fiscal responsibility key is to have the oversight and authorization of those funds come from an entity that isn't wearing a uniform and isn't as capricious as politicians.

The key also is to understand where the world is headed, how best to meet the threats that may arise, and not cling to strategies of bygone days. It would seem, that when you have the capability to essentially erase all life on the planet, you have achieved that position of strength. Is it still necessary to project power on theater-based platforms? Is it still necessary to maintain so large a conventional force? Is it wise to continue to upgrade weapons systems for a future world war? Because the next world war will be the last of everything. Forever.

Planning. Diplomacy. Treaties. Money. Intel. Obviously, these five tactics are employed already. However, where were all of these when America invaded Iraq a second time? The cost of that war as of early 2020 was $1.9 trillion[12]. Much like the Afghani War, (where there was a legitimate reason to fight), the result of invading Iraq will be a country in chaos when the United States pulls out.

The cost of war in the 21st century is simply too high. Despite enormous expenditures on Defense by the nations of the Earth, wars are no longer winnable. Defense **needs** to be about defending your own territory, not projecting power. The United States would still be the most powerful nation on the planet with a defense budget that was half of what it is now. $350 billion not spent on defense annually pays for much of the country's needs or begins to pay off the national debt.

President Dwight D. Eisenhower famously said in his farewell address, 'In the councils of government, we must guard against the acquisition of unwarranted influence, whether sought or unsought, by the military-industrial complex'. Too late.

The Defense Contract Management Agency (DCMA) is a Joint Chiefs of Staff designated Combat Support Agency comprised of approximately 12,000 civilian and military personnel, located in over 1,000 locations, managing approximately 309,000 active contracts with a total face value of $7.16 trillion of which $2.1 trillion has been obligated. Of the obligated amount, $303.2 billion remains un-liquidated. The Agency is a revenue generator for the Department, something very few Fourth Estate Agencies can claim.

-Defense Contract Management Agency Operation and Maintenance, Defense-Wide Fiscal Year (FY) 2021 Budget Estimates

The above, as seen through the eyes of any reasonable person, is completely beyond the pale of any logical explanation. President Eisenhower must be spinning in his grave. The audacity to claim that it is a 'revenue-generating' agency is a mockery of our Constitution. That revenue comes from *We, The People*. What level of congressional malfeasance, unwarranted influence, and bald-faced lying and theft has brought this nation to spend this kind of money to fight unwinnable wars?

Couple all of that with a really, slick advertising department that has convinced the American public that the most powerful nation in history is vulnerable, and you end up with bloated defense budgets, a lack of coherent national strategies, and corporations dictating national policy. You also end up with debt, shoddy infrastructure, and a government that serves the needs of corporations instead of its people.

There needs to be oversight, teamed with a hard-capped defense budget. Clear and concise strategic planning that comes from congress and spans administrations. A civilian/government entity that regulates procurement based on common sense solutions to *defending* the nation, not policing the world, feathering corporate nests, and seizing fossil fuels from Third World nations.

Law Enforcement and Crime

Its not about *defunding the police*, (worst phrase ever), its about *re-imagining the police*. Its about addressing the actual causes of crime, not continuing to pass laws that only feed a system that is designed to profit from repression.

The United States has less than five percent of the world's population, but about 25 percent of the prisoners. That number derives from about 2.2 million people in prison and the more than 11 million people who move through local jails each year. All at a cost of $80 billion every year. Meanwhile, 70 million people, about one-third of working age Americans, have some type of criminal record.[13] What is driving all this crime? How do we re-imagine law and law enforcement? What should the role of policing be?

There is simply no more difficult job than being a cop. Police officers are in the eye of every storm. Storms on the streets, storms in fiscal budget fights, storms in the media, and storms the police have created themselves. What was once a job *Andy Griffith* could do, has become a technical, tactical, bureaucratic nightmare.

Several factors have led to the state of policing the country is now in, and knowing these reasons is also the key to turning war officers back into peace officers and returning *to serve and protect* into the goal.

In the lust to gut government and privatize society, an exhausting list of poor policy decisions has crippled policing in America. Municipal and state budgets were stripped of funding. Social safety net programs were completely dropped. Outreach programs for the mentally ill and those suffering from dependency issues were defunded. Homelessness has increased as the gap between the haves and have-nots has widened. The lack of a health care system leaves holes in society where millions fall through each year. All of this has police officers tasked to perform an impossible job.

There is no possible way to expect an officer to protect citizens, enforce laws, act as a social worker, be an emergency medical technician, investigate crimes, and to do all of this inside a dizzying array of conduct codes and policies, understaffed, and with on average less than six months of training.[14] Cosmetologists have more training than the young people in America thrown onto the streets as police officers.

To rebuild trust between communities and police, stop extrajudicial killings of unarmed citizens, and make policing effective, society must first redefine the role of police officers. To ease the unreal expectations police officers have had placed on them, society needs to reprioritize social programs.

Likewise, the training to become a police officer needs to be more substantial and uniform across the country. Pivotal in this training is shifting the focus away from a 'siege mentality', in other words, having police understand that not all citizens are potential threats. The police need a clear role in supporting a community, as opposed to seeing a community as the enemy, or even worse, given the privatization of law enforcement and the prison system, the community as a cash cow.

The root causes of much of the street crime in America are systemically racist laws that go back to just after the Civil War. The politics of repression since reconstruction, the Jim Crow laws and redlining, have largely created the ghettoes where most crime takes place.

Aristotle said: 'Poverty is the parent of revolution and crime.' When presented with positive options, most people choose to succeed. When presented with dead-ends, hunger, and no future, people will do what they need to do to survive. In so doing, the cycle of repression, poverty, and crime goes on.

Here are some of the reasons that have created these dead-ends and the resulting crime: a lack of investment in schools and economic opportunity; draconian drug laws; bail policies that criminalize poverty; inadequate reentry services and employment discrimination against people who have been incarcerated; racial profiling; the for-profit prison system. Re-imagining the police goes hand-in-glove with making a just society based on equal rights.

Compounding this tilted field of justice, is that there is no centralized, codified national policy that sets the ground rules for policing. Correcting this would be a wonderful place to start. Setting down a standardized code of conduct, a strategic blueprint for supporting communities, and creating clean, clear channels of communication from the municipal level to the federal level, would create an even playing field for police and citizens alike. As an analogy, sports: it's hard to play the game when every referee interprets the rules differently.

Which brings us to this truism: as much as government wants the police to be a multi-tool, law enforcement is by nature rather two-dimensional: protect and serve. The siege mentality, quasi-military training that is being peddled in police academies only turns law enforcement into a hammer seeing all situations as nails.

In-order-to solve the issues of police brutality and high incarceration rates, the politics must be removed from the equation. The Department of Justice, coupled with a civilian team, and a congressionally appointed board, needs to create that standardized code of conduct, create a strategic national plan for policing, streamline the channels of communication not just between law enforcement at all levels, but also with the public. This commission can tap into ideas and philosophies in policing that are currently being pioneered in criminal justice programs at universities and think tanks across the nation.

Society needs to do its part as well. This includes funding police departments adequately through taxes, funding social programs and education, eliminating incarceration for many non-violent crimes, and providing positive options for those who are in the system to exit the system.

Addressing the systemic relationship between racism, poverty, and crime would solve most of the above listed issues. Crime is the indicator of something malignant below the surface. Treating the symptoms only causes the disease to spread. *Safety nets from poverty and springboards for opportunity:* this formula saves lives. Effective policing begins with logical laws, reasonable expectations, and trust between the public and the public safety officers.

Putting the badge on every morning is an honor. Taking the oath to protect and serve is a distinction. The law is a two-way street between the populace and the government. Law enforcement is tasked to police both. Not an easy proposition. Why make it more difficult, and more deadly, than need be.

Immigration, The Border, and The Wall

'The United States should be an asylum for the persecuted lovers of civil and religious liberty.'
-Thomas Paine

We are a nation of immigrants. America exists only because of immigration. It is the single strongest thread that runs through the history of the country. The more you limit immigration, the more you choke off the life-blood of America. As birthrates decline, as prosperity tempers the fires of inspiration and drive, immigration keeps alive the American spirit. Sadly, politics has oft used immigration and the Mexican border as a divisive issue, casting both in harsh light. As is so often the case in American politics, short-term political gain results in long-term misconceptions, while nothing is accomplished.

There is no question that the immigration process is a bureaucratic mess. Depending upon which center of the five is being applied to and depending upon which avenue to obtain citizenship is being utilized, it can take as few as six and a half months or as long as one hundred and twenty-three months[15] to be processed. As in any bureaucracy, there are numerous hoops to jump through. From the outside looking in, both as a citizen and as an immigrant, it looks like a confused mess. There is a process in place, but that process isn't always clear or straight forward.

Much of the confusion is when immigrants come into the country illegally or come to the border and seek asylum. Quotas for each way immigrants, asylum-seekers, and temporary workers may come to the United States are moved back and forth by Congress and the President. The processes to apply, who may apply, and how long that process will take, are also arbitrarily changed depending on which way the political wind is blowing. In addition to these issues, the detention centers and facilities to house refugees are woefully inadequate for the swell that has been rising at the southern border.

The unauthorized immigrant population hit a peak in 2007 at 12.2 million. That number has declined by about two million as of 2017 but is still dramatically higher than the 3.5 million in 1990[16]. The people who come to America's borders as refugees are essentially no different than immigrants who came to America in droves throughout the nation's history. They are fleeing strife, poverty, slavery, repression. They are seeking peace, opportunity, freedom, a fair shot at life.

Increasingly, a nativist movement has taken up the cry against immigration. In the short-term, it is simply another way to stoke fear in prospective voters. In the long term, it further muddies the waters of an issue that needs to be resolved.

In-order-to understand the drivers of that swell of refugees, one must look unflinchingly at the forest of issues. In a nutshell, conflict, poverty, and climate change are driving the number of refugees at the Mexican border. Drugs, cartels, American money for drugs, and the destabilized governments of Central America are the leading factors.

All of that is being driven by climate change as an exponent.

In the first place, it is the responsibility of those teetering governments to keep their citizens inside their borders. The reality of that statement is that governments that can barely keep the lights on are not going to be able to control their populace. As evidenced in the stories of America's past refugees, where there is a will, there is a way. Survival is a great motivator. Americans, and Europeans for that matter, must come to the realization that as more small nations of the world collapse, the tide of refugees is going to become a flood. Much of the cause of this collapsing lies with Western exploitation, persistent ethnic conflict, and climate-induced stressors on weak systems. That tide of refugees is already happening.

So, you want to build a wall. As a sovereign nation, America certainly has the right to protect and defend its border. The wall itself has been worked on since 1993[17]. During Donald Trump's four years as President, his promise to build the wall was a centerpiece to his presidency. At the end of four years, after 11 billion dollars was spent, 438 miles of primary and secondary wall had been built. However, only around 73 miles of wall had been built where no previous barriers had existed. The price per mile averaged out at 20 million a mile[18]. There is still some 800 miles of non-mountainous, primary border to be constructed[19]. The price tag for that, using the 20 million a mile average, is 16 billion dollars, or about 3 billion more than a Gerald R. Ford-class aircraft carrier.

The answer to this issue is quite simple and is, at the same time, quite humanitarian. Build the wall. Yes, static defense almost never works, but in this instance the wall is there to stem the flood of potentially hundreds of thousands of climate refugees. Dropping another 4 billion into improving the border centers that house asylum seekers, the detention centers, check points, and way stations, while working with the Mexican government to do the same on their side, further aids what is going to become a powder keg of a situation.

America needs to be honest with itself about what is happening there and why it is happening. The future push on the southern border is only going to intensify. This isn't about MS-13 and the flow of drugs. It is about a climate-driven catastrophe that is already playing out here and in Europe.

There first needs to be a cohesive, strategic policy set by congress that spans administrations. Then, by streamlining and significantly increasing funding for immigration, increasing the number of agents working for Customs and Border Patrol, finishing the wall, allowing a greater number of immigrants/asylum seekers to become citizens, this issue has a chance of being resolved.

The alternative to this solution is the standing army of the United States having to defend the border against starving, desperate climate refugees coming over in waves. *World War Z* at the Mexican border doesn't need to happen. The situation at the border worsens every day. This is not going to go away. Unbiased information creating coherent policy will help to avoid a horrific situation.

The Electoral College & The Filibuster

'Change is the law of life. And those who look only to the past or present are certain to miss the future.' -John F. Kennedy

James Madison on having a super-majority needed to pass legislation: 'the fundamental principle of free government would be reversed,' and 'It would be no longer the majority that would rule: the power would be transferred to the minority.'

In present-day, corporate America, from the bottom looking up, it appears as if the nation already suffers from minority-rule. In truth, the wealthy have held sway in the corridors of power since the first musket was fired at a Red Coat. The influence of industrialists, corporations, and money on the policies of the United States has always been abject and corrupt.

If America is to truly be what it says it is, a nation of the people, for the people, by the people, then eliminating two anachronistic structures from the political landscape needs to happen. The electoral college and the filibuster are quite simply standing in the way of getting anything done. The will of the people continually runs into these two walls. Furthermore, these structures were founded primarily because of slavery, reason enough to trash them both.

The electoral college was the confused result at the end of the Constitutional Convention of 1787. A system to elect the chief executive was needed. Many wanted congress to elect the president. Others wanted a direct popular vote. The resulting compromise was to have electors from each state, based on the number of representatives each state had, to elect the president based on the popular vote in each state. The problem arose with how to count slaves as part of the population. Similar, to the process of selecting how many representatives each state was allotted, it was agreed to have slaves count as 3/5 of a human. This argument was driven by the slave-holding states.

The Constitutional Convention became a group of tired, angry, frustrated men. Emotions were high, and patience was thin. The electoral college was born at the eleventh hour, protecting the slave-owning states from the non-slave states, protecting the anti-Federalists from the Federalists, and protecting everyone from mob rule and the fear that the public was too ill-informed to vote for president.

Everything in that last paragraph no longer exists. Slavery ended with the Thirteenth

Amendment. The people are informed. Mob rule, though it has been flirted with, has faced too many checks and balances, too much common sense and morality. The arguments between those seeking a strong central government, Federalists, and those seeking more power in the states, anti-federalists, is argued before, and determined by, each election.

What the electoral college does is disenfranchise millions of American votes for president. It gives too much power to states with less population. It means that voters in small, rural, less-diverse states have a greater vote than those in larger, urban, more-diverse states. The control/power/greed that comes with this equation is the only reason the electoral college is still tottering and drooling in the corner of every presidential election.

One human, one vote. Sure, sounds simple. The candidate with the most votes, wins. This isn't real heady stuff. Fair is fair.

Most importantly, the Electoral College is the avenue to overthrowing the Democratic Republic. It relies on the electors at the county and state level being immune from coercion, bribery, intimidation, and agent provocateur. Besides greed, why else is the electoral college still in place? Nostalgia and tradition, though charming, don't pay the bills. Eliminate the electoral college and return the power to the people. Eliminate the electoral college and shore-up the weakest point in the defense of our Democratic Republic.

'The histories of **the filibuster**, civil and voting rights, and race in America are intertwined,'

-Steven S. Smith, a political scientist and Senate specialist at Washington University in St. Louis.

A filibuster is a parliamentary procedure where one or more members of a legislature debate over a proposed piece of legislation to delay or entirely prevent a decision being made on the proposal. It is sometimes referred to as "talking a bill to death" or "talking out a bill" and is characterized as a form of obstruction in a legislature or other decision-making body[20].

The filibuster has been used as a tool to suppress the will of the people by a minority of senators since the early 19th century. Used primarily by Southern senators to block civil rights and voting rights, its legacy can be highlighted by Senator Strom Thurmond-Democrat, South Carolina, talking for over 24 hours attempting to kill the 1957 Civil Rights bill; and by Senator Mitch McConnell, Republican, Kentucky, to kill any bill that wasn't proposed by his party since 2007.

The filibuster was literally born by mistake in 1806, when senators absentmindedly deleted a rule that gave the majority the ability to cut off debate on a proposed bill. Used infrequently until the end of the 19th century, it was streamlined and made easier to employ in the 1970's, handing a minority of senators effective control over the nation. In this era of corporate money and influence in American politics, the filibuster is the tool of neo-liberalist-corporate America to effectively run the nation. Our Founding Fathers had intended for simple majority rule in the governance of the country.

'To give a minority a negative upon the majority (which is always the case where more than a majority is requisite to a decision), is, in its tendency, to subject the sense of the greater number to that of the lesser. The necessity of unanimity in public bodies, or of something approaching towards it, has been founded upon a supposition that it would contribute to security. But its real operation is to embarrass the administration, to destroy the energy of the government, and to substitute the pleasure, caprice, or artifices of an insignificant, turbulent, or corrupt junto, to the regular deliberations and decisions of a respectable majority.'

-Alexander Hamilton

America is a representative democratic republic. In this democracy, citizens vote for representatives to carry-out the business of the nation. That business is made possible through legislation-bills, that get voted on by our duly elected representatives and turned into law.

A simple majority in the House of Representatives passes the bill. This is called logic and is indicative of a democracy. The representatives voting for a bill, or against a bill, are, in theory, doing the will of the people.

In the Senate, a procedure known as cloture ends debate on a bill if there are 60 votes for the bill, thereby passing the bill. Cloture is a relic of British parliamentary rules. It is illogical and is not indicative of a democracy.

In fact, because of party politics, it gives the minority of senators more power than they should have, thereby grinding the business of the country to a halt. This is contrary to the will of the people, but largely in line with the corporate owners of those senators.

Of the People, for the People, by the People, doesn't exist until the filibuster is ended. The will of the people is in that simple majority. It is illogical, counterproductive, corrupt, and borderline fascist to have a minority of corporate lackeys running the most powerful nation on Earth. Destroy the filibuster and let the minority of senators bring a better argument on the issues to the people.

The Size and Role of Government

'The legitimate object of government is to do for a community of people whatever they need to have done, but cannot do at all, or cannot so well do, for themselves – in their separate, and individual capacities.'
-Abraham Lincoln

In 1776, sending a message across the Atlantic to Great Britain took on average seven weeks. Today it is instant. In 1776, the largest colony in America was Virginia with nearly three-quarters of a million people. Today there are eighteen cities with a higher population. The inflation-adjusted per capita GDP in 2019 was just above $65,000; in 1776 it was less than $2,000. Between 1775 and 1777, around one hundred thousand pounds of gunpowder was produced in the American colonies. One B83 thermonuclear bomb yields the equivalent of 1.2 megatons of TNT.

The world has evolved into a complex, striated, interconnected organism with the capability of ending all life on Earth. It would be beyond naïve to think that a loose confederacy of states would be anything more than low-hanging fruit for aggressors or simply a run of bad luck.

In order to *form that more perfect union, establish justice, insure domestic tranquility, provide for the common defense, promote general welfare, and secure the blessings of liberty*, a strong central government is needed. However, the strong central government cannot forget that they exist solely because the citizens allow them. The strong central government must also remember that the blessings of liberty are not just the personal freedoms we enjoy, but the rights to keep that strong central government in its place.

There is a great deal of gray area in this argument. In a nation of laws, when are there too many? In protecting the welfare and justice of some citizens, when do you infringe upon the rights of other citizens?

This may be an argument that can never resolve itself fully. And that might just be a good thing. By continuing to push and pull on this issue, we have returned to the lifeblood of democracy: intelligent debate on the nature of man, government, and freedom. There can never be a clear-cut winner in this debate. There isn't supposed to be. The energy created *by* this debate is as important as the debate itself.

At every election, the electorate goes to the polls and answers the question about the role of government in their lives. The natural American response to government is a healthy skepticism. That skepticism has been used to all-too-easily herd public opinion against common sense solutions to societal issues. The easiest way to do this is convince folks that taxes are too high, or that their personal freedoms are endangered. Why would someone want to do this? Follow the money.

It is vitally important to understand when the subject of 'too much government' is being employed to deregulate industries so they can profit at other citizen's expense, in other words: privatize the profits, socialize the losses. There needs to be shepherds. Without shepherds, laws, and agencies regulating the actions of citizens and their businesses, human nature guarantees that profit will be put before ethics.

Beneath the intellectual facets of the size and role of government, is a serious underpinning that does indicate the direction and style of the American government. The crux of this is who controls the nation: the People, or the wealthy-elite/corporations. The United States sits at a fork in the road: The Democratic-Republic we know and love, or a corporate-oligarchical dictatorship.

By being informed, by choosing common sense, by participating in the process, by doing the right thing for the greater good, democracy will prevail. By being swayed, for any of a dozen siren's songs being employed by the corporate elite, a divided America will allow itself to be sold.

This is not a nebulous, intellectual argument. This is being played out right now. This book has shone clear, harsh light on the practices being employed by a power-hungry few and the politicians/judges they own.

When laws are enacted, judicial decisions made, executive orders issued, ask yourself first, to whom does this profit? Then, how much is this going to cost? And who exactly is paying for this? If it's the citizens who are paying for it, and the wealthy-elite/corporations are profiting from it, then the role of government has failed. Corporate subsidies are an excellent example of when neo-liberalists support government overreach. Deregulation of toxic industries is another. Again: privatize the profits, socialize the losses.

Our Founding Fathers argued endlessly over how strong the central government should be, and how much influence it had over our daily lives. This argument continues. It's supposed to.

Protecting freedom is essential. Protecting the weak from the strong creates an even playing field. Life, liberty, and the pursuit of happiness deserves shepherds. As issues come up, laws are how a nation-of-laws responds. Common Sense, unbiased courts, and an informed electorate is what guides the process. Where there is overreach, in time it will be curtailed; where there are egregious actions, in time laws will be enacted. What is important is to keep the conversation ongoing and civil. What is important is to know when that argument is being employed for profit, power, and corruption.

Separation of Church and State

In 1956, the United States of America changed its motto from *e pluribus unum*, (out of many, one), to *In God We Trust*. Our founding fathers may still be aghast. They understood how divisive, corrosive, and volatile connecting religion to politics is. The 1st Amendment reads as thus:

Congress shall make no law respecting an establishment of religion, or prohibiting the free exercise thereof; or abridging the freedom of speech, or of the press; or the right of the people peaceably to assemble, and to petition the Government for a redress of grievances.

It is more than clear that a wall exists to separate government and religion while allowing for the citizens to practice religion. Thomas Jefferson and James Madison had clear and strong feelings on this subject. Much of their belief in the separation of church and state derives from the philosophies of Roger Williams, a puritan minister who founded what would become Rhode Island. Williams had stated that there needs to be a 'hedge or wall of Separation between the Garden of the Church and the wilderness of the world'.

James Madison went on to state: 'Congress should not establish a religion, and enforce the legal observation of it by law'. He also said, 'practical distinction between Religion and Civil Government is essential to the purity of both, and as guaranteed by the Constitution of the United States'.

Thomas Jefferson had this to say on the matter: '*...no man shall be compelled to frequent or support any religious worship, place, or ministry whatsoever, nor shall be enforced, restrained, molested, or burthened in his body or goods, nor shall otherwise suffer on account of his religious opinions or* *belief; but that all men shall be free to pro-fess, and by argument to maintain, their opinion in matters of religion, and that the same shall in no wise diminish enlarge, or affect their civil capacities.'*

And, *'Believing with you that religion is a matter which lies solely between Man & his God, that he owes account to none other for his faith or his worship, that the legitimate powers of government reach actions only, & not opinions, I contemplate with sovereign reverence that act of the whole American people which declared that their legislature should "make no law respecting an estab-lishment of religion, or prohibiting the free exercise thereof", thus building a wall of sep-aration between Church & State.'*

In the beginning of the nation's history, many of the colonists had fled a Europe where religious tolerance didn't even exist between different Christian sects. It is im-portant to remember that less than 130 years separates the birth of America and the Thirty Years War. A war fought between Protestants and Catholics that resulted in the deaths of between 3 million and 12 million people. Religion has been a primary tool/weapon in the hands of authoritarian governments to exert their will over their people and to conquer other people. Unbridled passion, be it blind faith or patriotism, is a recipe for genocide.

The Founding Fathers understood this and incorporated two key clauses that American Law uses to protect and separate the Church from the State, the Establishment Clause and the Free Exercise Clause: *Congress shall make no law respecting an establishment of religion, or prohibiting the free exercise thereof.* It is the very first line of the 1st Amendment of the Constitution. *That* is how important it is to both the Church and the State. *That* is how important the separation of the two is to keep the Democratic Republic, a democratic republic.

So, given how important the separation of Church and State is, and how ardent our Founding Fathers were on this issue, what happened in 1956 to change the nation's motto from one that is inclusive, to one that is not only exclusive, but flies in the face of the Constitution? The Red Scare of the 1950's and an overreaction by fear mongering politicians. Hoping to distinguish America from communist Russia, Congress, who were seeing communists behind every curtain, passed a law making the change. This switch of mottos still enjoys wide-spread support, even as numbers of practicing church-goers dwindles. The importance of separating Church from State is being lost in continued fear mongering, and the use of Evangelical Christians as a voting bloc. There is a great deal of truth in the old saying: *when fascism comes to America, it will be wrapped in a flag and carrying a cross.* Sadly, that image continues to be branded and packaged with increasing frequency.

In 1970, in Aronow v. United States, the Ninth Court of Appeals judged, solely on the opinion of the judge, that the motto did not establish a religion, that the case need not be tried. The terms "patriotic" and "ceremonial" have been used in-regards-to this case and with prayer in public schools. The merits of prayer, God, and religion of any kind aside, even a first, baby step over the hedge or wall separating Church and State is one too many. The demise of our Democratic Republic can happen quite quickly when passions are stoked with the firebrand of religion. There are numerous examples throughout mankind's less than moral history of nations using religion to repress their own citizens or incite their citizens to wreak atrocities. It would be blind to think it couldn't happen here. The stacking of the Federal courts with uber-conservative, hyper-religious judges may very well be a means to win votes but be warned: religion has a sneaky way of destroying common sense and replacing it with '*the End Justifies the Means*'.

E Pluribus Unum, was established as the motto on the Seal of the United States in 1782 by an Act of Congress. Thus, it should remain the motto of these United States in all applications. The wall that separates Church and State was placed there by our forefathers for a reason, breeching that wall is an existential threat to these United States. James Madison: 'The purpose of separation of church and state is to keep forever from these shores the ceaseless strife that has soaked the soil of Europe in blood for centuries.'

Anyone trying to incorporate religion into politics has an agenda and should be viewed as a threat. Our Founding Fathers were adamant on this.

Flashpoints. They don't seem so big and bad when they are rationally discussed. They don't seem so insurmountable when people set emotions aside, objectively look at data sets, and make logical decisions.

What cannot happen with these divisive issues is to *not* deal with them. Passing the mess onto the next generation because it is too politically scary, and career threatening, only makes a bigger mess. In some cases, that mess is strategically detrimental to the welfare of the nation.

If not dealing with these issues is the height of irresponsibility, using them as a tool to divide the country, stoke fear, and reap profit from the chaos, is evil. The next two chapters dovetail along these very lines.

CHAPTER TWELVE

Tales of Brave Ulysses

'If we are to have another contest in the near future of our national existence, I predict that the dividing line will not be Mason and Dixon's, but between patriotism and intelligence on the one side, and superstition, ambition, and ignorance on the other.'
-President Ulysses S. Grant
Annual Reunion of the Army of the Tennessee in Des Moines, Iowa, on Sept. 29, 1875.

So, here we are, in an America that is sharply divided along the lines that President Grant warned us about nearly 150 years ago. In an America where objective data and irrefutable information are jettisoned for conspiracy theories and outright lies. In an America where the ambitions of a fossil fuel-minted aristocracy stack the courts, buys-off legislators, and openly lies to their fellow citizens.

In a plot twist that even Shakespeare could not have penned, it is the Republican Party that has become the bastion of this duplicity. The Party of Presidents Lincoln and Grant, the party of abolitionists, the party that had stalwartly defended the Constitution, now uses those principals as window dressing, as a sales pitch.

Since before the Civil War, the Republican Party was so staunchly anti-slavery that it wasn't possible for the party to field candidates in elections south of the Mason-Dixon line. It was the Democrats that represented the Southern Aristocracy. From Antebellum through the Civil War, during Reconstruction and the Jim Crow laws, right up to the 1960's, the Democrats stood shoulder to shoulder with the basest elements of Southern society, KKK included. That ended when Northern Democratic Senators and Democratic President Lyndon Johnson pushed the Civil Rights Bill. It was then, as the Democratic Party embraced those initiatives, and

President Johnson continued the policies of President Franklin Roosevelt, that Southerners turned from the Democratic Party.

In the resulting vacuum, as Northerners fled the Rust Belt to Southern cities, as once sparsely populated, rural states became more powerful, the Republicans seized the opportunity. Much of the money fueling this came from conservative sources, from captains of industry who, embracing Movement Conservatism and Neo-liberalism, found in this opportunity a fountain of support, and a wall of obstruction to any progressive ideas. All that was needed to cultivate this fertile ground, was to play the Race Card.

The result became a Republican Party that attempts to win at all costs; that obstructs instead of compromises; and has essentially auctioned off control of the country to industry, particularly, the fossil fuel industry.[3]

What the Republicans didn't see coming, nor anyone else, was Donald Trump. The ground had been poisoned to perfection for the advent of a populist, quasi-fascist movement to spring forth. America had been laced with thirty-plus years of Hate Radio and disinformation. The Microphone was booming a diatribe that appealed to white, working-class people who had been abandoned as manufacturing jobs disappeared. The Race Card was being played. The anti-immigration card was being played. The Culture Wars were invented. Yes, the divisions in American society were carefully cultivated.

Donald Trump is no fool. A man who has lived his entire life in exploiting everything around him, he quickly recognized the well springs of public feelings and the emotive divisions they cause. Once the target population is recognized, the playbook has been written many times over, most expertly by Adolf Hitler. The comparison between President Trump and Adolf Hitler is President Trump's in doing. How so? Hitler's speeches were bedside reading for Mr. Trump[4], and his own Joint Chief of Staff, General Milley, had to warn his aides in January of 2021, that an impending 'Reichstag' moment could happen and that the defeated President Trump might throw a coup. General Milley went on to refer to Trump as a "classic authoritarian leader with nothing to lose," and then he compared the former president's actions to those of Nazi leader Adolf Hitler[5].

Once again, in the ensuing vacuum created by Trump as the old-guard Republicans were caught flat-footed, a host of characters seeking power coat-tailed with the soon-to-be president creating a Republican Party light years removed from Lincoln and Grant. The 'Reichstag' moment may still be looming on the horizon. The number of swastikas and Confederate flags flying at Trump rallies should be warning enough.

'If fascism comes…it will be wrapped in the American flag and heralded as a plea for liberty and preservation of the Constitution.'
-James Waterman Wise Jr.

'By using propaganda skillfully, any delusion can become fact.'
-Michael Corthell

'Why, America's the only free nation on earth. Besides! Country's too big for a revolution. No, no! Couldn't happen here!'
-Sinclair Lewis from, *It Couldn't Happen Here.*

President Ulysses S. Grant has been smeared throughout the years by the descendants of the very people he helped to crush. Contrary to the lampooned, alcoholic he has been portrayed as, his presidency was one of the most pivotal for America. He, President Lincoln, and the Republican Party, led this country through its darkest hours. They did this with strength and courage, with empathy and honesty, with integrity and grit. The near defeat of the United States, and history as we know it, quite literally came down to the left flank of the Union army on the second day of the Battle of Gettysburg.[6] Once again, citizen soldiers defended democracy from autocracy and slavery.

America stands today at a very perilous place. The *Big Round Top* of the Battle of Gettysburg we are faced with is a concerted effort to undermine and erode the institutions of democracy. As the 20th Maine protected the left flank then, we are called upon now, to recognize the ongoing actions taking place to overthrow these United States.

What is it we are faced with? Nothing less than a coup d'état of the Democratic Republic we love. In order, to *truly,* hold onto the Constitution, to honor our Founding Fathers and the brave men and women who made the ultimate sacrifice in defense of that Constitution, we must hold the line.

Who is it we are faced against? A populist uprising comprised of white nationalists, anarchists, confederates, fascists, and extreme right-wing militias, that have usurped/coalesced with the basest elements of the new Republican Party. These groups have rallied around the cult of personality of Donald Trump. They are fueled by monies from big oil, from tens of millions of 'followers', and from billionaires who share the same philosophy of a white-centric, one-party, Christian America[7].

'The job facing American voters…in the days and years to come is to determine which hearts, minds and souls command those qualities best suited to unify a country rather than further divide it, to heal the wounds of a nation as opposed to aggravate its injuries, and to secure for the next generation a legacy of choices based on informed awareness rather than one of reactions based on unknowing fear.'

-Mitt Romney, Republican Senator and Governor

The Promise we make as Americans has never been needed more. It requires each of us to look inward and be brutally honest with ourselves: What ethics do I truly, believe in? What values do I hold dear? What freedoms do I want for myself, and do I wish to extend to my fellow citizens? And am I willing to fight for these beliefs?

Our answers to ourselves cannot be duplicitous. They cannot be hypocritical. These questions are difficult. The answers may be painful. In the end, it isn't the trials we face, but how we face them. How we come back from the difficult journey is what defines us. Not wealth. Not status. Not how we dominate, but how we unite.

This great war for the soul of America cannot be fought without America's conservative voice. Without the Republican Party or some entity that represents what President Lincoln and President Grant exemplified, the struggle to preserve the United States of America as our Founding Fathers intended is doomed. Without that unending energy created by many different philosophies debating, struggling, and coming together, the Nation dies.

Somewhere in the wilderness that has become the American Republican soul, exists voices of responsible, clear-headed, common sense, conservative thought. Unclouded by greed, by lust for power, by the machinations of billionaires hiding their ambitions and twisted plans behind the philosophy of Neo-liberalism.

The Republican elected officials of America must pull themselves away from the abyss. They must search their souls deeply and find a courage that conservatives have not had since President Eisenhower. They must ask themselves whom do they really represent: the Constitution, conservatives, and Americans? Or the special interests of the corporate elite?

To be a conservative in America in 2021 is knowing you have no voice in your nation's capital; that no one has your back. To be a conservative in America in 2021 is to have been stabbed in the back first by the Republican Party selling out to the fossil fuel industry, and secondly selling out to a demagogue. Either of these paths is an express elevator to authoritarian government terminating the Party and the Country.

It does not have to end this way. There are voices of reason on the right side of the aisle desperately trying to be heard. Voices that are trying to be crushed by the fascists. Voices who embody the bravery that once was the Party of Lincoln and Grant.

'Extremes to the right and left of any political dispute are always wrong.'
- Dwight D. Eisenhower

Elections are won in the middle. It is moderate voters that decide elections. Those folks listen to both sides. They listen to reason. They compromise. Stripping them of free access to, and upending fair elections, will only serve to stir-up an American hornet's nest. The slumbering giant in American politics are the millions of American voters whose chests beat with patriotism, justice, and a yearning to be free. These folks are watching and listening.

Two quotes from President and General Ulysses S. Grant:

'There never was a time when, in my opinion, some way could not be found to prevent the drawing of the sword.'

'Nations, like individuals, are punished for their transgressions.'

America's transgressions are plain for the world to see. The nation is still largely divided by that terrible Civil War. It has taken nearly one hundred and sixty years before Confederate statues were taken down. When Baghdad fell during the second Iraq war in 2003, Saddam Hussein's statue was one of the first things to be destroyed.

It is important to understand that the slave-holding states were staunchly anti-federalist, and that the current Republican 'Red Wall' is built on those same states. The drive for State's Rights and autonomy allows individual states to work outside the parameters of ethics and morals. The slew of draconian, illogical laws passed in Texas in the summer of 2021 is an example, as are the voter suppression laws being enacted in similarly oppressive states.

The fuel behind this is not a political or philosophical movement; it is not the defense of the Constitution and Civil Liberties. It is the same power grab by the same Fossil Fuel Corporations and the ambitious, greedy men who own them. The division of America allows the status quo to keep the fires of carbon-belching industry going. Since World War II, as the American Empire embraced a level of unprecedented wealth, the Corporate Elite have been leaning on the thermostat. Despite knowing what science was telling them, despite knowing what all this industry was doing to the environment, they continued to do the opposite of common sense, to disregard the greater good.

The industrialized world has been living life like a slam dance and treating the Earth like a mosh pit. The piper is calling to be paid. Answering that call will strip power and influence from a handful of conspiring and greedy men.

Not answering that call may just strip the Earth bare.

'So: global warming is the ultimate problem of oil companies because oil causes it, and it's the ultimate problem for government haters because without government intervention, you can't solve it. Those twin existential

threats, to cash and to worldview, meant that there was never any shortage of resources for the task of denying climate change.'
 -Bill McKibben

'I want you to act as if our house is on fire. Because it is.'
 -Greta Thunberg

CHAPTER THIRTEEN

Forewarned *Was* Forearmed

Through the course of this book, we have deftly avoided the 51 billion-ton, extremely rabid gorilla in the room. Other than explaining the need for a wall on the southern border, *World War Z* happening live on your television, Climate Change has largely been ignored in the text of this book until now. The gorilla, 51 billion-tons is the average amount of greenhouse gasses we pump into the atmosphere each year[1], simply is not going to go away, and because of the enormity of the threat it poses, demands the next to last chapter in this book.

For over forty years, America has frittered away at doing anything substantial about one of the greatest existential threats to the nation's national security. There are reasons for this blasé attitude, psychological, sociological, political, and economical, but evidence, knowledge, and awareness among scientists have not been among them.

We have known about greenhouse gasses and a warming planet since John Tyndall, an Irish physicist, in 1859, figured out that because carbon dioxide molecules absorb heat, the greater their concentration in the atmosphere, the more likely that there would be changes in climate.[2] This led the Swedish chemist Svate Arrenius in 1896, to deduce that the burning of coal and petroleum for energy could raise global temperatures.[3] In 1965, President Lyndon Johnson commissioned a study which warned of rapid melting in Antarctica, rising seas, increased acidity of fresh waters, changes that could not be controllable at any level of government.[4]

In 2015, the world gathered in Paris for the United Nations Climate Change Conference. The target of the Paris Agreement that was signed at that conference is to hold global temperature rise to below 2 degrees Celsius. The United Nations Environmental Programme, in their annual Emissions Gap

Report in 2019, stated that even if countries meet their commitments to the 2015 Paris Agreement, the world is headed for a 3.2 degrees Celsius global temperature rise over pre-industrial levels.

The last time the earth was three degrees warmer was during the Pliocene, three million years ago, when beech trees grew in Antarctica, the seas were eighty feet higher, and wild horses galloped across the Canadian coast of the Arctic Ocean.[5]

So, with all this knowledge, with Presidential commissions, Congressional commissions, independent studies, with hard research producing hard data, why has so little been done to avoid disaster?

In 1957, Humble Oil, the predecessor to Exxon, published a study on the relationship between the burning of fossil fuels and the enormous amount of carbon that had been injected into the atmosphere. Twenty years later, after funding more research, conducting more 'in-house' studies, and now staring the Charney Report, a 1979 watershed study on carbon and climatology, in the face, Exxon had a different question to ask in its own research: how much of the warming could be blamed on Exxon. In other words, public relations, and profit trumped humanity.

Between 2000 and 2016, the fossil fuel industry spent more than 2 billion dollars to defeat Climate Change legislation.[6] Presidents Reagan and Trump, kings of deregulation and incapable of understanding the science evolving around them, stole precious time. Right-wing radio politicized Climate Change creating denial in a large swath of the population. After the 2020 election, in the brewing clown-storm created by the Republican Presidential candidate who was defeated, even Charles Koch decried his involvement in helping to create so polarized a political arena.[7]

It is more than ironic that this individual would bemoan the state of politics in America. He, his brother, and ultimately his father, have shaped the American political environment to their own profits and ambitions. This thread that runs through this book, the Koch's, and other oligarch's manipulation of American democracy, deserves to land right here in a chapter entitled, *Forewarned Was Forearmed*, that has to do with Climate Change. Their lobbying, their pseudo-think tanks, their false-science, their jilted-studies, their bankrolling the Senate, the House, the Supreme Court, along with those entities in the individual States, has brought us to a place where esteemed naturalist David Attenborough had this to say:

'If we continue on our current path, we will face the collapse of everything that gives us our security…Our duty right now is surely to do all we can to help those in the most immediate danger.'

The watch word in 2021, and one that the fossil fuel industry has latched onto, is adaptability. That it is already too late and all we can do is cope with whatever outcomes there are. This is the final nail in the coffin. Recognizing a problem is halfway to solving it, as the old saying goes. Getting populations to understand this, and to vote for humans that are proactive in addressing this nightmare of a problem, is the key.

So much is this the key, that voting rights are being threatened all over the United States. At the time of this writing, the *For The People Act, HR 1*, passed in the House of Representatives, was set to die in the Senate.

A recording of a communication from wealthy Republican donors, quite literally said to Senate Minority leader Mitch McConnell that the only way to defeat this bill would be to use the filibuster. Mind you, over 60% of the country supports the passage of HR 1. The person at the center of this malfeasance is Charles Koch, who's organization *Stand Together* was already delivering talking points against the bill to politicians and like-minded media.[8] In the words of Thomas Jefferson:

'The end of democracy and the defeat of the American Revolution will occur when government falls into the hands of lending institutions and moneyed incorporations.'

The World Health Organization estimated in 2014, that Climate Change would lead to about 250,000 additional deaths each year between 2030 and 2050, from factors such as malnutrition, heat stress and malaria.[9] That estimate was based on data that has since been shown to be quite conservative. In a recent study by NASA, it was shown that the Earth is trapping twice as much heat as it did in 2005.[10] Even if we use the 2014 WHO estimates, the death toll in that 20-year span is 5 million.

There is a strange and morbid similarity between Fred Koch, the father of Charles and David Koch, selling the process to make advanced aviation fuel to the Nazi's, and his son's buying American energy policy, the Climate Change response of the nation, and the ability of the people to vote for politicians whose efforts would be counter to their profits and ambitions. To be sure, the Koch brothers are not alone in owning congress, the courts, and the tilted playing field, but they designed and built the system to pervert democracy.

In their defense, what are the odds that the rise in global temperatures is natural, and not caused by mankind's burning of fossil fuels? Those odds would be 1 in 3.5 million, or 0.00003%[11].

Now, even if we were to capture all the carbon tomorrow, place it in pods, and jettison it into the Kepler Belt of asteroids, that is just the largest head of the monster born from our affair with industrialization. Species loss, eco-system collapse, pollution, plastic pollution, topsoil degradation, aquifers drying up, the acidification of the oceans, the slowing down of the ocean's great conveyor, ozone depletion, overuse of fertilizers, deforestation, these are equally stacked against us. To slay the beast, we must address them all. In fact, many of them are related, as is the response to solving these issues.

So, how do we go about pulling off a global version of David vs. Goliath? By electing people with the brains to understand what we're up against, the integrity to not be purchased, the will to see it resolved, the fearlessness not to be afraid to fail, and the courage to keep on trying. Because the risk of continuing to do nothing is the end of America, the end of civilization, and quite possibly the end of our species. That's what's at stake.

In order, to avert the worst of Climate Change, we will need to come together as a species on a planet-wide basis. Even as Climate Change drives us apart via population movement, wars, poverty, starvation; even as old hatreds are rekindled due to deprivations; we must stand together.

America is in a unique place in this fight. As a nation, we have produced more CO^2 than any other country since 1751, about 25% of all emissions, or over 400 billion tonnes.[12]

This weights us with a tremendous amount of responsibility. We are also the one nation standing with the resources to go toe-to-toe with Climate Change. As we did in World War II, we can take the lead, fire-up the brains and the brawn, and go get this done.

'The truth is: the natural world is changing. And we are totally dependent on that world. It provides our food, water, and air. It is the most precious thing we have, and we need to defend it.'
-David Attenborough

The force multiplier for the bad guys is that the human population will probably top 10 billion by 2060. The World Footprint Network states that currently, we use 1.6 Earths to provide the resources we use and absorb our waste. By 2030, if consumption trends continue at the current pace, we will need 2 Earths.[13] The estimated world population in 2030 is 8.6 billion. Nearly all that consumption, by all those people, is fueled by fossil fuels pumping carbon into the atmosphere.

In 2007, the Center for Strategic and International Studies labelled their comprehensive climate report, 'The Age of Consequences'. We are well down that road, and the bridge has nearly been washed-out. There are no words to express how dire the situation is. It is immensely, difficult to understand something that is unseen, and so pervasive that everything seems normal, much less fight it. Yet, here we are, in-the-midst of a fight few of us can comprehend, and all of us are in. And this time, it's for keeps.

The good news is that all the technologies we need, already exist. Save for cold-water fusion, which could be coming in the next decade[14], there are enough tools in the tool-shed to get to zero emissions and start capturing carbon. We have all the resources we need save one: the political will to make this happen.

If you're looking for divine intervention, it is already here. The human mind, the invention of whatever creator you wish to believe in, is singly the most phenomenal thing on our planet. When coupled with human determination, human desire, and a need to adapt and survive, well, we're kind of unstoppable.

'The time for doing what we can has passed. Each of us must now do what is necessary.'

-Christiana Figueres, UN Executive Secretary for Climate Change and Tom Rivett-Carnac, Senior Political Strategist for the Paris Agreement, co-authors of *The Future We Choose.*

'I recall the old fisherman's prayer: The sea is so large, Lord, and my boat is so small…We face the prospect of being trapped on a boat we have irreparably damaged, not by the cataclysm of war but by the slow neglect of a vessel we believed to be impervious to our abuse.'

-President George H.W. Bush

'At no point since complex life appeared on Earth has so much carbon been released as quickly as we are releasing right now.'

-Mark Lynas. *Our Final Warning: Six Degrees of Climate Emergency.*

'We are the first generation to feel the sting of climate change, and we are the last generation that can do something about it.'

-Jay Inslee

'A man is seated on top of a tree in the midst of a burning forest. He sees all living beings perish. But he doesn't realize that the same fate is soon to overtake him also. That man is a fool.'

-Lord Mahavira (6th century BCE)

'How could I look my grandchildren in the eye and say I knew what was happening to the world and did nothing.'

-David Attenborough

'We do not inherit the earth from our ancestors. We borrow it from our children.'

-Native American Proverb

CHAPTER FOURTEEN

Outro

'The cause of America is in great measure the cause of all mankind.'
-Thomas Paine

America. The dream. The idea. The freedom. The promise it holds, and the promise we make to America itself.

Freedom from, freedom for, and the inherent promise we each make that ensures freedom for all those around us.

Freedom for the opportunity to live life according to our own principles; to achieve that which we each considers successful; to have the opportunity for life, liberty, and the pursuit of happiness.

From many, one. Many, as in *all* of us; one, as in *together*. One nation, indivisible. Each of us is the firewall to keep this nation undivided. Each of us, while yearning to be free, also shines the light of liberty for our fellow citizens and citizens to be.

The *United* States of America. The nation of immigrants. The nation represented by every color of the rainbow. The nation built upon an idea: *That All People Are Created Equal.* A nation founded on an idea must work to uphold that idea. Unlike any other form of government before America, that idea is the focal point of our Nation. It is nebulous, hard to hold, easily lost. Easily stolen.

'The price of Liberty is eternal vigilance.'
-Thomas Charlton.

A powerplay has been in action by vain and aspiring men to usurp this democracy in favor of a system of government that empowers and enriches the few at the expense of the many. Because of the perpetual greed and ambition of the few wolves, there are shepherds to protect the flocks. The Constitution establishes this: *In Order to form a more per-*

fect Union, establish Justice, insure domestic Tranquility, provide for the common Defense, promote general Welfare, and secure the Blessings of Liberty, laws are enacted, people and property are protected, the rights of every citizen are marked as hallowed by these very laws. A strong central government is needed to ensure that protection, to provide for the common good, to assist in moving the country coherently forward.

'The legitimate object of government, is to do for a community of people, whatever they need to have done, but cannot do, at all, or cannot, so well do, for themselves in their separate, and individual capacities.'
-Abraham Lincoln

That government exists because the citizens allow it. The citizens, remaining vigilant, must see to it that the government isn't bought and sold by the few wolves. The citizens have at their recourse all manner of rights to ensure this does not happen. Among those are free speech, the right to assemble, the ability to boycott, and most importantly, the right to vote in free and fair elections.

Critical thinking skills, disseminating information, being vigilant, and being skeptical is the best recourse to recognize whom the wolves are. The wolves will only rarely appear as wolves. The wolves will come dressed as politicians, as businessmen, as preachers, as scholars, talking heads, and even as soldiers and cops. They have their own tools of disinformation, discord, divisiveness, and treachery. They have the engines of commerce and manufacturing. They have vast sums of money.

What they don't have is our loyalty. Or our numbers. And most importantly, the collective industry and buying power of 330,000,000 people.

Standing at this most pivotal time in America's history, standing at the fork of the road between the Democratic Republic our Founding Fathers intended, and the oligarchical dictatorship that is being orchestrated, the decisions we make as a nation in the next few years will determine the future of our country and the world.

The issues of national security, of democracy, of sustainable economy, of a nation that strives to protect its citizens, all of this comes down to now.

In order, to provide that most important American ideal, a better future for our children, we will need to make sacrifices. We will need to look hard at how we live our lives. How we vote. From whom we purchase goods and services. We must evaluate what is truly important in a human lifetime and act upon that reflection.

We will need to understand when we're being ripped-off. When we're being lied to. Even if those lies have been carefully wove into the fabric of generations of lives. We will use deductive reasoning, inductive reasoning, and Occam's Razor. We will follow the money from deep corporate pockets to legislative and judicial slush funds, to bogus think tanks and Political Action Committees. We will follow the money from Foundations whose interests are purely to perpetuate the Corporate coup, even if the names of those Foundations seem as if they are in the People's best interests: Citizens United, The Heritage Foundation, American Family Association, Americans For Prosperity, The Heartland Institute, etc. By doing all this we will understand fully who is perpetuating the thievery and the lies.

If a man came to your home, poisoned your yard, your water, your food, your air; took your hard-earned money with empty promises; stole your land for his friends; and then continued to ask for your support; you'd beat him into next week. That is what is going on writ large in America by men saying they are defending your rights, saying they are defending the Constitution.

It is no mystery why this nation's First Amendment rights are being stripped away. Without free and fair elections, without the right to assemble, without the ability for workers to organize, without legal protections for small business, without a legal system devoid of political bias and built upon the principle of justice-for-all, without some sort of Fairness Doctrine shepherding the incessant flow of polluted information, then what seems like the only recourse for The People is violence.

That is quite simply unacceptable on all levels. Isaac Asimov once said, 'Violence is the last refuge of the incompetent.' This is not the time to lock and load. It is the time to come together. We have at hand many tools of activism. Henry David Thoreau once said, 'Disobedience is the true foundation of liberty.' We cannot allow hatred to divide and destroy us, but let those passions empower us. It is time for Americans to be that man with only a briefcase standing in front of the tank.

This moment in time is critical. An America torn apart at this junction in human history will terminate civilization. If we continue as individuals to vote for personal needs, a robust economy based on outdated models, lower gas prices, distracting single issues, or other whimsical notions, then we are effectively playing Russian Roulette with all six chambers loaded.

The Doomsday Clock as of January 27th, 2021, stands at 100 seconds to midnight. This is the closest to midnight it has ever been.

'Humanity continues to suffer as the COVID-19 pandemic spreads around the world. In 2020 alone, this novel disease killed 1.7 million people and sickened at least 70 million more. The pandemic revealed just how unprepared and unwilling countries and the international system are to handle global emergencies properly. In this time of genuine crisis, governments too often abdicated responsibility, ignored scientific advice, did not cooperate, or communicate effectively, and consequently failed to protect the health and welfare of their citizens.'

-Bulletin of the Atomic Scientists

This distinguished body went on to explain that though the Covid-19 Pandemic was not an existential threat to mankind, it showed the massive, canyon-like cracks in the world's ability to process, organize, and defend civilization in a time of great crisis. It then highlighted the three greatest threats to our species: climate change, nuclear weapons, and next-generation weapons.

America, the country that quite literally won two world wars, is still failing in real time against Covid-19 as these words are written. Many of the caustic threads hemorrhaging democracy listed in this book are precisely why this failure is happening. Nature doesn't care how you vote, your opinion, where you get your information, or any other aspect of your life. Nature does exactly what it wants to, when it wants to, and there is very little humanity can do to prevent it.

'This is one of those moments where we have to decide who we are as a country. Are we 300 million people who happen to live in the same place? Or are we fellow Americans who recognize we're stronger when we care for and protect one another? If we do this together, we will turn this pandemic around.'
-US Surgeon General Dr. Vivek Murthy

By ignoring, dismissing, or denying the math, science, and facts as Nature presents them, we are allowing this nation to be governed by unreasonable, greedy men who will stop at nothing to own everything, who are leveraging their fortunes with a dystopian tomorrow.

So, here we stand. Backs to each other, cleverly divided, played against one another, watching the shiny, distracting objects while our wallets are being lifted, our rights are being stripped, and our children's future is being auctioned off.

This book is a klaxon-call for America to unite and move forward as one people. Our Founding Fathers left us with all the tools we need. Science, critical thinking, education, and our own initiative, industry, and fortitude will provide the dynamic force. Our collective will, yearning to be free, provides the fuel.

With reason, we succeed. With compromise, we proceed. With common sense, we prevail.

Cooperation will prove to be many times more important than competition. In the past, when one neighbor needed a barn built, the community came together, and they raised that barn. It is in this selfless spirit that we must move forward.

We are in the fight of our lives. Fighting right now for democracy, for the Democratic Republic we love. We are in a fight for the future of civilization, for the very existence of our species. We are heroes, one and all. We are each of us, nineteen feet tall.

'You cannot shake hands with clenched fists.'
-Indira Gandhi

'Injustice anywhere is a threat to justice everywhere.'
-Martin Luther King

'From everyone who has been given much, much will be demanded; and from the one who has been entrusted with much, much more will be asked.' -Luke 12:48

'The greatest illusion is that mankind has limitations.'
-Robert A. Monroe

'Justice and truth are the common ties of society.'
-John Locke

'I hope I shall possess firmness and virtue enough to maintain what I consider the most enviable of all titles, the character of an honest man.'
-George Washington

'I like the dreams of the future better than the history of the past.'
-Thomas Jefferson

'Resolution is our inherent character, and courage hath never forsaken us.'
-Thomas Paine. Common Sense.

'It's the message that's important, not the messenger.'
-Rodney 'Gypsy' Smith

This book is the culmination of over twenty years of research. Files bulging with notes scribbled on all manner of napkins, papers, and post-its, were sorted and placed in new files that would eventually become the chapters. As the select bibliography shows, many books were read on political philosophy, economic philosophy, history, ethics, and biographies of the individuals who put the greater good, common cause, and passion for the human spirit over personal interest. Hundreds of articles in all manner of journals were read as well. This book to some extent has occupied one-third of my life.

The book took about one year to write. In the process of writing the book, new inspirations shattered old beliefs, current events highlighted past transgressions and triumphs, and head-shaking astonishment would sometimes be followed by a wry smile. Much was learned, as much was discarded.

I truly believe we can manage the crises before us; that we can overcome the existential threats to the planet, our species, democracy, and America. If I didn't believe in the tremendous capability of my fellow Americans, of the enduring human spirit, of the infinite possibilities blooming on the horizon, then trust me, I would have spent the past twenty years in more Bacchanal pursuits.

Always remember *The Promise* you make to yourself, to your fellow Americans, and to the country. Stay engaged. Stay positive. And most importantly, *stay together!*

Godspeed, and God Bless America!

CHAPTER NOTES

Chapter One-Intro

1. Definition of Insane Greed. AlterNet. Julia Conley. 9/16/19

1. The Seven Deadly Sins of American Politics: Greed.Ozy. Sean Braswel. 9/27/16

1. Greed, Ethics, and Public Policy. Brookings. Alice M. Rivlin. 3/16/2003

1. Politics Won't Cause the Fall of America, Greed Will. Odyssey. Andrew Padovano. 5/13/19

2. 2017 Tax Law Tilted Toward Wealthy and Corporations. Center on Budget and Policy Priorities.

2. How Corporate Lobbyists Conquered American Democracy. The Atlantic. Lee Drutman. 4/20/15

2. Citizens United Explained. Brennan Center For Justice. Tim Lau. 12/12/19

2. 91 Major US Companies Paid Zero Federal Taxes Last Year Thanks to the GOP Tax Law. The American Independent. Oliver Willis. 12/16/19

2. Nearly Half the Pentagon Budget Goes to Private Contractors. The American Conservative. William D. Hartung. 10/11/17

3. Nine Charts About Wealth Inequality in America. Urban Institute. 10/5/17

3. What Wealth Inequality Looks Like: Key Facts and Figures. Federal Reserve Bank of St. Louis. Ana Kent, Lowell Ricketts, Ray Boshara

<u>Chapter Two-Common Sense</u>

1. Common Sense. Thomas Paine. Dover Edition. 1997

2. Thomas Paine and The Promise of America. Harvey J. Kaye. Pg. 43. Hill and Wang. 2005

3. Common Sense. Thomas Paine. Dover Edition. 1997

4. Common Sense. Thomas Paine. Dover Edition. 1997

5. Supreme Court Decisions pages. Citizens Take Action Website

<u>Chapter Five-Uncommon Sense</u>

1. Common Sense. Thomas Paine. Dover Edition. 1997

2. Democracy. Wikipedia. 2021

3. Republicanism. Wikipedia. 2021

4. Liberalism. Wikipedia. 2021

5. Libertarianism. Wikipedia. 2021

6. Neoliberalism. Wikipedia. 2021

7. Socialism. Wikipedia. 2021

8. Common Sense. Thomas Paine. Dover Edition. 1997

<u>Chapter 6- The Dark Side</u>

1. Dark Money. Wikipedia. 2021

2. Dark Money. Jane Mayer. Pg. 37. Anchor Books.2016/2017

3. John Birch Society. Wikipedia. 2021

4. American Industrialist Koch Helped Build the Nazi's WW 2 Refineries, Did His Sons Betray the World? Glen Hendrix. Medium.com. 12/31/19

5. Meet Rebekah Mercer, the deep-pocketed co-founder of Parler. Alexis Benveniste and Kaya Yurieff. CNN. 11/16/20

6. Redmap. Wikipedia. 2021

7. Texas vs Pennsylvania. Wikipedia. 2021

<u>Chapter 7- Better Angels</u>

1. Countries That Give the Most to Charity. World Atlas. World Facts. Oishimaya Sen Nag. 6/6/19

2. Wage Stagnation in Nine Charts. Economic Policy Institute. L. Mishel, E. Gould, J. Givens. 1/6/15

3. The Complexities of Raising the Minimum Wage on the Retail Industry. NPR. Alina Selyukh. 2/8/21

4. Raising the Minimum Wage to $15 an hour: What the Research Says. Journalist's Resource. Clerk Merrefield. 11/14/19

5. G.I. Bill Wikipedia. 2021

6. The Average Salary by Education Level. SmartAsset. Amelia Josephson. 5/15/18

7. The Economic Benefits of Education. The Borgen Project. Roberto Carlos Ventura. 7/2/18

8. Universal Health Care Can't Work in the U.S. Due to Size. Fact/Myth. Thomas De Michele. 6/28/17

9. 3 Reasons the U.S. Doesn't Have Universal Health Care. US News and Report. Timothy Callaghan. 10/26/16

10. The Rising Cost of Health Care by Year and Its Causes. The Balance. Kimberly Amadeo. 10.17/20

11. Why Do WE Need to Reform US Health Care. The Balance. Kimberly Amadeo. 10.30/20

11. www.health.gov.au About Us. The Australian Health System.

11. Pros and Cons of Universal Health Care. Formosa Post. 6/8/21

12. Most Americans Favor a National Health Plan. CBS News. Fred Backus, Jennifer De Pinto. 10/15/19

13. Movement Conservatism. Wikipedia. 2021

13. The End of an Era: Movement Conservatism Gets Real. Bill moyers.com. Heather Cox Richardson. 8/16/17

14. Families in Poverty. USA Facts. 2021

15. Federal Safety Net Welfare Budget 2019/2020

16. This Is What Minimum Wage Would Be If It Kept Pace with Productivity. Center For Economic and Policy Research. Dean Baker. 1/21/20

17. Movement Conservatism. Wikipedia. 2021

18. The Global Decline of Manufacturing. Statista. Katharina Bucholz. 7/9/20

19. US GDP by Year. The Balance. Kimberly Amadeo. 7/30/20

Chapter 8-Capital Radio

1. Yellow Journalism. Wikipedia. 2021

2. FCC Fairness Doctrine. Wikipedia. 2021

3. How Pro-Trump Forces Pushed a Lie About ANTIFA at the Capital Riots. New York Times. Michael M. Grynbaum. Davey Alba. Reid. J. Epstein 3/1/21

Chapter Nine- Grassroots

1. Government. Colonial. In British America. Encyclopedia.com. Cengage 3/8/21

2. 6 Facts About US Political Independents. Pew Research. John Laloggia. 5/15/19

3. Distributism. Wikipedia. 2021

4. Centesimus Annus. 1991 Encyclical. Pope John Paul II.

Chapter 10- Free and Fair

1. 67 Percent of Americans Support HR1 For the People Act. www.dataforprogress.org 1/22/21

2. Just 20% of US Adults say they Trust the government in Washington to "do the right thing" just about always or most of the time. Pew Research Center. 9/14/20

3. Revealed: Conservative Group Fighting to Restrict Voting Tied to Powerful Dark Money Network. The Guardian. Sam Levine. Anna Massoglia. 5/27/20

4. Nine Election Fraud Claims, None Credible. FactCheck.org. Saranac Hale Spencer. 12/11/20

4. Director Chris Krebs, US Cyber Agency Explains Why President Trump's Claims of Election Interference are False. 60 Minutes. Scott Pelley. 11/30/20

4. Addressing Modern Threats to the Integrity of Free Elections. Fortinet. Jim Richberg. 11/19/19

5. Judge. Wikipedia. 2021

6. Demographics and Composition of the 117th Congress. American Bar Association. 1/27/21

6. 2 Charts That Show Just How Old Congress Actually Is. CNN. Chris Cillizza. 1/29/21

7. Opinion: Amy Coney Barret's truly scary association. CNN. Paul Begala. 10/10/20

8. Democratic Lawmakers Demand Amy Coney Barret Withdraw Dark Money Case Involving Group That Backed Her Confirmation. Forbes. Alison Durkee. 4/20/21

<u>Chapter 11-Flashpoints</u>

1. 2 in 3 Support Stricter Gun Control Laws. The Hill. John Bowden. 4/14/21

2. A Doctor's Insights into Gun Violence and Gun Laws Around the World. NPR. Marc silver. 8/6/19

3. 7 Facts About Guns in the US. Pew Research Center. John Gramlich and Katherine Schaeffer. 10/22/19

4. Just 3% of Americans Own More than Half the Country's Guns. Big Think.com. Paul Ratner. 2/18/18

5. Calculate the value of $300,000 in 1956. Dollar Times. 2021

6. Record Debt and Inequality Gap? Its Almost Like 40 Years of Republican Tax Cuts Failed. USA Today. Steven Strauss. 10/3/19

7. What Is the Federal Gas Excise Tax Rate? The Balance. Rachael Morgan Cautero. 9/17/20

8. The Composition of Federal Revenue has Changed Over Time. Tax Foundation. Erica York and Madison Mauro. 2/28/19

9. Corporate Tax Breaks Cost US Government $180 Billion per Year: GAO Report. Huff Post/Reuters. 4/15/13

9. Corporate Tax Breaks and the Federal Budget. National Priorities Project.

10. The US Spends More on Defense than the next Ten Countries Combined. Peter G. Peterson foundation. 5/15/20

11. US Military Spending/Defense Budget 1960-2021. Macrotrends.

12. The Iraq War has cost the US nearly $2 Trillion. Military Times. Neta C. Crawford. 2/6/20

13. Why are Incarceration Rates in the US So High Relative to Other Countries? Forbes. Valerie Jarrett on Quora 7/1/16

14. The Institute for Criminal Justice Training Reform.

15. Immigration Application Processing Times. Immigration Help.org. Johnathon Petts, ESQ. 10/7/20

16. Unauthorized Immigration Population in the United States from 1990-2017. Statista. 5/4/20

17. A Brief History of the US Border Wall. Yahoo Politics. Caitlin Dickson. 8/31/15

18. Biden Halts US-Mexico Border Wall Construction, Trump Made Dismal Progress. Market Realist. Dan Clarendon. 1/26/21

19. Trump Ramps Up Border Wall Construction Ahead of 2020 Vote. Washington Post. Nick Miroff and Adrian Blanco. 2/6/20

20. Filibuster. Wikipedia. 2021

<u>Chapter 12-Tales of Brave Ulysses</u>

1. Jefferson's Attitudes Toward Slavery. www.monticello.org

2. Jefferson and Slavery. theheritage.org

3. The Republican Party of Obstruction: Disturbing and Distressing. Huff Post. Lance Simmens. 3/18/10

3. The Republicans' Unprecedented Obstruction by the Numbers. Crooks and Liars. John Perr. 10/13/11

3. A Walk Down Memory Lane of Republican Obstructionism. Washington Monthly. Nancy LeTourneau. 2/1/15

3. Oil and Gas Has Pumped Millions into Republican Campaigns. The Guardian. Suzanne Goldberg and Helena Bengtsson. 3/3/16

3. How Republicans Rig Elections. Republicans Exposed.

3. Lee Atwater Set the Bar for Republican Lies and Obstruction. Lee Atwater's Secret Papers. The New Yorker. Jane Mayer. 5/7/21

3. Republicans Ratchet Up Fossil Fuel Insanity. Clean Technica. Steve Hanley. 6/14/21

3. Republicans Preview Months Ahead Filled with Obstruction and Extremism. CNN. Stephen Collinson. 7/8/21

4. Donald Trump Kept Book of Adolph Hitler's Speeches in His Bedside Cabinet. Independent. Benjamin Kentish. 3/20/17

5. Book: Joint Chiefs Chairman Fretted Over Coup Attempt After Trump Lost 2020 Election. The Gazette. Jake Dima. Washington Examiner. 7/15/21

6. The Killer Angels. Michael Sharra. Ballentine Books. 1974

7. Oligarchy in America. How the Republican Party Perfected the Techniques of the Rule of the Few. The Atlantic. Jack Beatty. 3/2005

7. Trump Has Turned America into a One-Party State. The Federalist. David Harsanyi. 8/3/16

7. Fossil Fuel Industries Pumped Millions Into Trump's Inauguration, Filing Shows. Inside Climate News. Marianne Lavelle. 4/19/17

7. The Republican Plan for a One-Party State. The Washington Spectator. Rick Perlstein. 9/6/17

7.The GOP's Laboratories of Oligarchy. The New Republic. Matt Ford. 12/4/18

7. Confronting White Supremacy. Michael C. McGarrity. Assistant Director, Counterterrorism Division, Federal Bureau of Investigation. 6/4/19.

7. George Will: GOP Has Become a 'Cult' of Trump. The Hill. Justin Wise. 6/5/19

7. Big Oil Remedies 'Friend' Trump with Millions in Campaign Funds. The Guardian. Peter Stone. 8/9/20

7. The Supreme Court's Religious Persecution Complex. The New Republic. Katherine Stewart. 4/9/21

7. Uniting for Total Collapse: The January 6 Boost to Accelerationism. Combating Terrorism Center at West Point. Brian Hughes and Cynthia Miller-Idriss. April/May 2021. Volume 14. Issue 4.

7. Top Law Enforcement Officials See the Biggest Domestic Terror Threat Comes from White Supremacists. The New York Times. Eileen Sullivan and Katie Benner. 5/12/21

7. The Christian Right is in Decline and its Taking America with It. The New York Times. Michelle Goldberg. 7/9/21

Chapter 13-Forewarned Was Forearmed

1. How to Avoid a Climate Disaster. Bill Gates. Alfred A. Knopf. 2021

2. Losing Earth. Nathaniel Rich. MCD. 2019

3. Losing Earth. Nathaniel Rich. MCD. 2019

4. Losing Earth. Nathaniel Rich. MCD. 2019

5. Losing Earth. Nathaniel Rich. MCD. 2019

6. Losing Earth. Nathaniel Rich. MCD. 2019

7. Charles Koch Regrets His Partisanship. The Hill. Kaelan Deese. 11/13/20

8. Inside the Koch-Backed Effort to Block the Largest Election-Reform Bill in Half a Century. The New Yorker. Jane Mayer. 3/29/21

8. Behind Closed Doors, Republican Plutocrats Conspiring Against Democracy, Let the Mask Slip. Jacobin. Luke Savage. 4/14/21

9. More Than 250,000 People May Die Each Year Due to Climate Change. Live Science. Rachael Rettner. 1/17/19

10. Earth is Trapping Twice as Much Heat as it Did in 2005. Space.com. Tereza Pultarova. 6/24/21

11. Our Final Warning: Six Degrees of Climate Emergency. Mark Lynas. 4th Estate. Harper Collins. 2021

12. Who Has Contributed the Most to Global CO_2 Emissions? Our World in Data. Hannah Ritchie. 9/1/19

13. Surviving The 21st Century. Julian Cribbs. Springer International Publishing. Switzerland. 2017

14. America's First Nuclear Fusion Reactor Could go Online in 2025. The Motley Fool. Rick Smith. 10/11/20

Chapter 14-Outro

1. The Big Money Behind the Big Lie. Jane Mayer. Article in The New Yorker. 8/2/21

SELECT BIBLIOGRAPHY

This bibliography was compiled by going through my library, checking my notes, and sifting through the chapters. It is in no way alphabetical or coincides with the flow of the book. Nor is it complete. The idea for this book was well over two-decades before the time of its writing, and a great deal of source material was unearthed and read, resulting in folders overflowing with papers. These are the books that provided the greatest insight.

The two greatest tools we have as humans are books and meditation. A substantial amount of both went into *Uncommon Sense*.

Common Sense. Thomas Paine. Dover Edition. 1997

The Declaration of Independence

The Constitution of the United States of America

The Selected Political Writings of John Locke. Edited by Paul E. Sigmund. W. W. Norton & Company. 2005

The Great Law of Peace of the Longhouse People (Iroquois) (League of Six Nations). Dekanawidah and Hiawatha. Akwesasne Notes.

The Unfinished Revolution: A Concise History of the American People. 2nd Edition. McGraw-Hill. 1997

Benjamin Franklin's The Art of Virtue. Edited by George L. Rogers. Choice Skills. 1996

1776. David McCullough. Simon and Schuster. 2005

America Afire. Bernard A. Weisberger. HarperCollins. 2000

The Soul of America: The Battle for Our Better Angels. Jon Meacham. Random House. 2018

Team of Rivals: The Political Genius of Abraham Lincoln. Doris Kearns Goodwin. Simon & Schuster. 2005

With Malice Toward None: A Life of Abraham Lincoln. Stephen B. Oates. Harper & Row. 1977

The Wealth of Nations. Adam Smith. Bantam Classics.

Das Kapital. Karl Marx. Wordsworth Editions Limited. 2013

The Republic. Plato. Penguin Classics.

The Portable Machiavelli. Edited and Translated by Peter Bondanella and Mark Musa. Penguin Books. 1979

Leviathan. Thomas Hobbes. Edited by Richard E. Flathman and David Johnston. W. W. Norton & Company. 1997

Meditations. Marcus Aurelius. Dover Publications. 1997

The Politics of Jesus. Obery M. Hendricks, Jr. Three Leaves Press. 2006

Bury My Heart at Wounded Knee: An Indian History of the American West. Dee Brown. Henry Holt and Company. 1970

The Prize: The Epic Quest for Oil, Money & Power. Daniel Yergin. Simon & Schuster. 1991

The Great War for Civilization: The Conquest of the Middle East. Robert Fisk. First Vintage Books Edition. 2007

The Art of Peace. Morihei Ueshiba. Translated by John Stevens. Shambhala Publications Inc. 1992

The Art of War. Sun Tzu. Translated by Thomas Cleary. Shambhala Publications Inc. 1988

Sapiens: A Brief History of Humankind. Yuval Noah Harari. HarperCollins. 2015

1491: New Revelations of the Americas Before Columbus. Vintage Books. 2005

Dark Money: The Hidden History of the Billionaires Behind the Rise of the Radical Right. Jane Mayer. Penguin Random House. 2016

Distributism Basics: An Explanation. David W. Cooney. Practical Distributism. 2013

The Third Way. Pope Blessed Leo XIII and Gilbert K. Chesterton. Veritas Splendor Publications. 2012

The Servile State. Hilaire Belloc. 1912. Cavalier Books. 2018

Small Is Beautiful: Economics as if People Mattered. E. F. Schumacher. Harper & Row. 1973

The Future We Choose: Surviving the Climate Crisis. Christiana Figures & Tom Rivett-Carnac. Manilla Press. 2020

Our Final Warning: Six Degrees of Climate Emergency. Mark Lynas. 4th Estate. 2020

The Uninhabitable Earth: Life After Warming. David Wallace-Wells. Penguin Random House. 2019

Losing Earth: A Recent History. Nathaniel Rich. Penguin Random House. 2019

Collapse: How Societies Choose to Fail or Succeed. Jared Diamond. Penguin Books. 2006

Surviving the 21st Century: Humanity's Ten Great Challenges and How We Can Overcome Them. Julian Cribb. Springer International Publishing. 2017

All Hell Breaking Loose: The Pentagon's Perspective on Climate Change. Michael T. Klare. Henry Holt and Company. 2019

The Rise and Fall of the Third Reich. William L. Shirer. Simon and Schuster. 1960

Why We Lost: A General's Inside Account of the Iraq and Afghanistan Wars. Daniel P. Bolger. Houghton Mifflin Harcourt Publishing Company. 2014

The Killer Angels. Michael Shaara. Random House. 1974

April Morning. Howard Fast. Bantam Books. 1962

The Hero Code. Admiral William H. McRaven. Grand Central Publishing. 2021

Democracy Needs to Find the Will to Roar. Heather Cox Richardson. Article quite easy to find and heartily recommended. 12/30/20

The Anishinaabe Code of Ethics.

ABOUT THE AUTHOR

Liam Sean is a writer, musician, actor, graphic artist, and chef who dwells deep within the Boreal Forests of the Upper Great Lakes. For projects & info, please wander to www.liamsean.com

www.ingramcontent.com/pod-product-compliance
Lightning Source LLC
Chambersburg PA
CBHW071612030726
47598CB00001B/240